Scene on the road near Walker, Minn.

HELD UP

M-86—Moonlight Scene

NO. 18. NEW BRIDGE OVER MISSISSIPPI RIVER, FORT S

MINN.

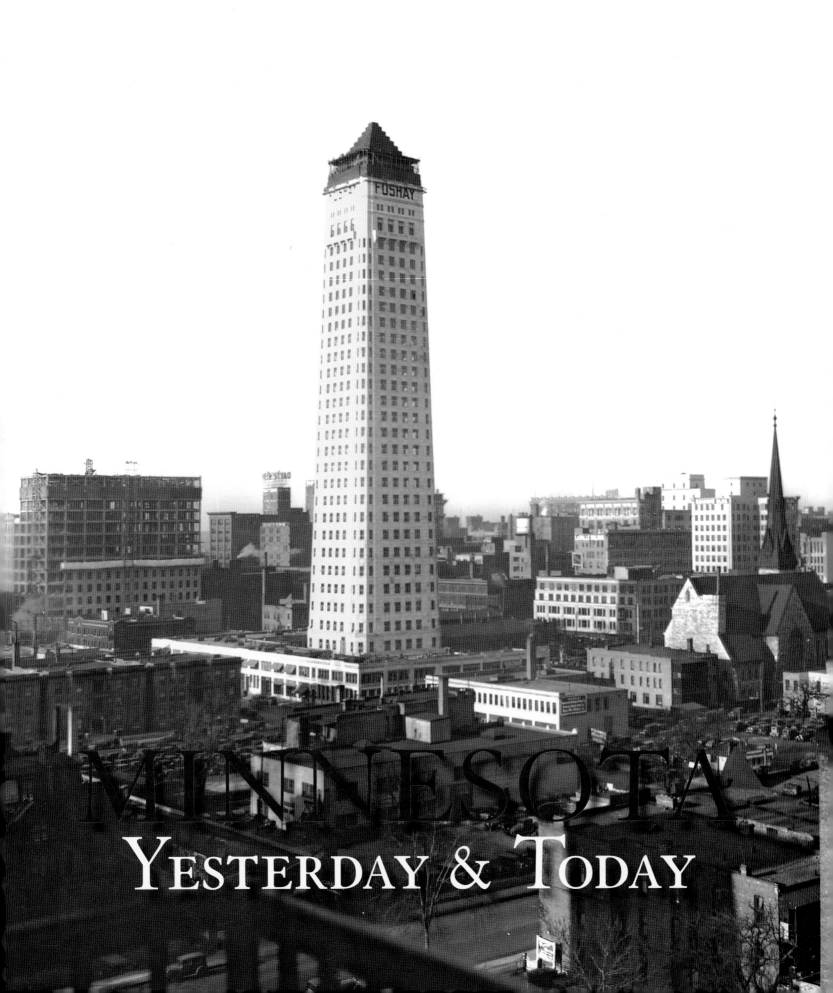

MINNESOTA
YESTERDAY & TODAY

Photographs by **Layne Kennedy**

Text by **Greg Breining**

Voyageur
Press

First published in 2006 by Voyageur Press, an imprint of MBI Publishing Company, Galtier Plaza, Suite 200, 380 Jackson Street, St. Paul, MN 55101-3885 USA

MBI Publishing Company titles are also available at discounts in bulk quantity for industrial or sales-promotional use. For details write to Special Sales Manager at MBI Publishing Company, Galtier Plaza, Suite 200, 380 Jackson Street, St. Paul, MN 55101-3885 USA

ISBN-13: 978-0-7603-2641-1
ISBN-10: 0-7603-2641-X

Editor: Michael Dregni
Designer: Julie Vermeer

Printed in China

Library of Congress Cataloging-in-Publication Data

Kennedy, Layne, 1957-
  Minnesota yesterday & today / photography by Layne Kennedy ; text by Greg Breining.
    p. cm.
  ISBN-13: 978-0-7603-2641-1
  ISBN-10: 0-7603-2641-X (hardcover)
  1. Minnesota--History--Pictorial works. 2. Minnesota--Pictorial works. I. Breining, Greg. II. Title. III. Title: Minnesota yesterday and today.
  F607.K39 2006
  977.60022'2--dc22
                    2006015607

On the Frontispiece:

On the frontispiece: A dogsled races by an Indian pictograph overlooking Saganaga Lake in the federal Boundary Waters Canoe Area Wilderness. The rock art of the Anishinabe (also known as Chippewa or Ojibwa) adorns many cliffs in northeastern Minnesota. Painting with iron oxide mixed with a gluey binder rendered from fish such as sturgeon, Indian artists depicted human forms, canoes, celestial objects, animals, and supernatural creatures. What do the pictographs mean? Selwyn Dewdney, a once-pioneering Canadian student of northern pictographs, suggested that "to all appearances, the aboriginal artist was groping toward the expression of the magical aspect of his life." Anthropologist Thor Conway writes in *Painted Dreams*: "The soul speaks in the language of images and symbols."

On the Title Pages:

On the title pages: When the 448-foot Foshay Tower was built (shown here nearly complete in 1928), it towered above all else in Minneapolis. Indeed, it was the first skyscraper built west of the Mississippi and it remained the tallest building in Minneapolis until 1971, when the IDS Tower (left) soared to 792 feet. Other prominent features of the city's skyline are the cream-colored Wells Fargo Center (774 feet) and the haloed 225 South Sixth (776 feet).

Yesterday's photos: Minnesota Historical Society

Acknowledgments

A big round of applause goes out to editor Michael Dregni, who brought this project to life with a strong sense of direction and energy. His dedication to ensuring coverage with a statewide balance was unwavering and his time sorting through a sea of historical imagery enthusiastic. Writer Greg Breining brought vast experience and knowledge of the state and his location advice was indispensable.

A warm thanks to all the wonderful folk I met along this journey. I acquired valuable knowledge from each of you that I will forever store in my mental toolbox.

Thanks as well to Tracey Baker at the Minnesota Historical Society for all of her assistance.

Finally, a thanks to my wife Martha and our kids Croix, Brooks, and Austin, who at times traveled with me, practicing both patience and participation, and for their understanding when I had to travel solo. I never forget the times we spend together.

Layne Kennedy
Minneapolis 2006

Introduction

I recall long ago the first time I heard someone refer to Minnesota as a "prairie state." I don't recollect who said it, or the context of the remark, but I remember my reaction. No, it's not, I thought, it's a woodland state. I had spent the summers of my life in a cabin in north-central Minnesota surrounded by lakes and forests of aspen, birch, pine, and spruce. Of course Minnesota was a woodland state.

Later I came to realize that Minnesota is both—and more. Considering how little up and down we have—Minnesota has no mountains to speak of—there is surprising variety. We are at an ecological crossroad. Prairies creep in from the south and west, leafy woodlands flow from the east into the heart of the state, and somber boreal coniferous forests enter from the northeast.

The variety goes beyond the physical. A friend of mine, then a columnist and editorial writer for the *St. Paul Pioneer Press*, once remarked that "Minnesota is a liberal state full of conservative people." The great influx of immigrants from Scandinavia, Ireland, Germany, Slavic countries, and elsewhere—added to a population that already included American Indians, African Americans, French, and British—created a society with strong communitarian leanings, with occasional flashes of social conservatism. We see it play out in our politics today: We vote overwhelmingly Democratic but still send Republicans to the Senate. We are perceived as overwhelmingly liberal, but foster a strong pro-life movement. And while we have elected only two women to the U.S. House of Representatives, we have sent a professional wrestler to the governor's mansion. Our pedigree, and presumably our social predilections, are becoming more complex all the time, as Hmong, Somali, Ethiopian, and Mexican Americans join the community.

The state's complex and contradictory portrait is revealed in the photography of *Minnesota Yesterday & Today*. I'm sure the historical photos will bring back nostalgic recollections of Minnesota as it once was. I'm sure also that the modern photos by my friend Layne Kennedy will make you marvel at how far we've come—and at how some things remain the same.

Many things about the old Minnesota were comforting and good—from the network of family farms across the land, to neighborhood theaters on the streets, to mom and pop resorts in the north woods. While it saddens any lifelong Minnesotan my age to see such things become scarcer, I can't help but be intrigued and excited by the changes in our society and by the new ideas and interesting customs that changing times and new people bring to our state.

Greg Breining

Indians gathering wild rice in Minnesota   C-2739

WILD RICING

In late summer, Anishinabe harvest wild rice from shallow lakes and quiet streams of northern Minnesota. Over the years, birch-bark canoes have given way to plank boats (in the postcard, from about 1939), and then to modern canoes of aluminum, fiberglass, or plastic. Methods have otherwise changed little. The sternman (or "poler") propels the canoe with a long push-pole. The "beater," sitting amidships, draws the rice heads over the gunwale with one "knocker" and sends the ripe kernels into the canoe with the other. On a good day, poler Jeffrey Bellecourt and beater Bob Libby can gather more than 300 pounds. Harvested rice is sun-dried or parched in a kettle, thrashed by foot, and winnowed with a birch-bark basket (as Catherine Gwinn demonstrated in this 1937 photo). The yearly harvest of *manomin*, or "good berry," is the echo of centuries past.

Today, wild rice is also grown on land and harvested by combines—a far cry from the ways of the past.

Yesterday's photos: Minneapolis Public Library; Minnesota Historical Society

WITCH TREE

narled and forlorn, northeastern Minnesota's most famous tree has stood on Hat Point on the Grand Portage Indian Reservation for perhaps 400 years. Known as *Manitou Geehigaynce*, Little Spirit Cedar, the twisted northern white cedar was a familiar landmark to early Anishinabe canoeists and French-Canadian voyageurs, who left offerings of tobacco at its base to ensure safe passage on Lake Superior. The practice persists today. The tree became familiar to non-Indians through the efforts of Minneapolis artist Dewey Albinson, who coined the common name Witch Tree. Sometime later, about 1965, Hollywood-style Indians posed with the tree. Recently, the Grand Portage band has purchased the site where the tree stands on to prevent the land from being developed.

Yesterday's photo: Minnesota Historical Society; Voyageur Press archives

PUB. BY J. H. AUSTIN, DEALER IN AND MFGR. OF PIPESTONE CURIOSITIES.

PIPESTONE QUARRY

In an undated postcard, Indians pause in their work at the quarries of southwestern Minnesota. Since ancient times, members of many tribes traveled to the quarries to dig the soft carvable rock, prized for various effigies and ornamentsand especially for ceremonial pipe bowls, for which the material was named *pipe*stone. Trade carried pipestone across the continent.

In 1836, artist George Catlin, for whom pipestone was named catlinite, recorded this Dakota legend of the stone's origin: "The Great Spirit, in the form of a large bird, stood upon the wall of rock and called all the tribes around him, and breaking out a piece of the red stone formed it into a pipe and smoked it, the smoke rolling over the whole multitude. He then told his red children that this red stone was their flesh, that they were made from it, that they must all smoke to him through it, that they must use it for nothing but pipes: and as it belonged alike to all the tribes, the ground was sacred, and no weapons must be used or brought upon

it." Wrote nineteenth-century explorer John Wesley Powell: "It is not too much to say that the great pipestone quarry was the most important single locality in aboriginal geography and lore."

Native Americans, mostly from local Dakota tribes, continue to work the quarries, now part of Pipestone National Monument. Travis Erickson (white shirt) and Todd Tellingheusen wield sledges to break and excavate the hard Sioux quartzite, in order to expose the thin layer of soft pipestone that angles ever deeper into the earth. Quarrying must be done with hand tools and muscle; no power tools allowed. Only Native Americans may quarry.

Traditionally, craftsmen carved many different styles of pipes. Simple tubes evolved into elbows and discs. One design popular throughout the plains was the T-shaped "calumet." It was often used in ceremonies, so European settlers came to call it a "peace pipe." This horse-head pipe is based on traditional animal-effigy designs.

Yesterday's photo: Voyageur Press archives

CANOE BUILDING

Anishinabe craftsmen build a birch-bark canoe at a camp in about 1895. For centuries, woodland tribes such as the Anishinabe harvested large sheets of bark from standing birch trees, sometimes sewing together smaller pieces of bark with the split root of black spruce. They drove stakes into the ground to form a frame, and then laid in the bark, inside out, to form an upright canoe hull. Later, they would add wooden ribs, gunwales, and thwarts. Finally, they would seal the seams with spruce gum tempered with charcoal and tallow.

Woodland Indians traveled the continent's waterways in their birch-bark canoes. For cross-country travel, there was nothing to rival these boats—a fact European explorers soon realized. French-Canadian voyageurs paddled 36-foot-long cargo canoes across the Great Lakes, and ventured far inland with more portable 25-foot bark canoes.

Unfortunately, with the disruptions to the Indians' way of life, the skills and knowledge necessary to build birch-bark canoes near-ly vanished. It might have disappeared altogether but for the book *The Bark Canoes and Skin Boats of North America* by Edwin Tappan Adney and Howard Chapelle, along with the devoted study and work of a handful of Indian and non-Indian craftsmen.

One of the builders who sustained the bark canoe through its dark ages was the late Bill Hafeman, shown here in his workshop in Bigfork. Hafeman gathered materials for his boats from the woods along northern Minnesota's Big Fork River. His students, among them Jack Minehart, have sustained the craft and tradi-tion, even as birch bark has been replaced by a plethora of new materials in canoe-building.

Among these new high-tech craft are lightweight and stream-lined models made of Kevlar, fiberglass, and carbon fiber by canoe-racer Mike Cichanowski, owner and founder of We-no-nah Canoe in Winona. Essential to the exploration and development of Minnesota, the canoe continues to be a vital craft here.

Yesterday's photo: Truman Ward Ingersoll, Minnesota Historical Society

Stockade
Grand Portage, Minn

GRAND PORTAGE

This reconstruction of the Grand Portage trading post stands on the shore of Lake Superior, probably just a few years after it was built in 1938. More than 200 years ago, this site on the Grand Portage Indian Reservation had been one of the busiest centers of transcontinental trade west of the Appalachians. Scottish partners of the North West Company established the post to carry on trade that linked Europe to the front range of the Rockies and to the northernmost reaches of the boreal forest in Canada. Each summer, Grand Portage was the meeting place of North West agents; of French Canadian voyageurs bringing cloth, kettles, and iron goods across the Great Lakes; of canoemen known as "winterers" carrying furs from the interior of Canada; of independent traders; of Anishinabe; and of African Americans who worked in the fur trade as slaves or canoemen. At the summer "rendezvous," wrote Alexander Mackenzie in 1801, "there are sometimes assembled to the number of 1,200 men indulging themselves in the free use of liquor and quarreling with each other."

A strengthening American nation pressured the North West Company to move to Canada. In 1802, the company salvaged the timber and abandoned the Grand Portage site. More than 130 years later, the Civilian Conservation Corps funded a survey of the old foundations and artifacts, along with a reconstruction of the main hall and palisade. The site was designated a national historic site in 1951, and a national monument in 1958. The first reconstruction was struck by lightning and burned down in 1969, but the buildings were soon rebuilt.

Today, Grand Portage National Monument consists of a palisade, the hewn-log Great Hall, and an adjoining kitchen with a gaping fireplace. Tables are set as if the Scottish partners are about to arrive. Women bake fresh bread in the outdoor oven. Re-enactors in an "Ojibwa village" construct a birch-bark wigwam. Staff members stage musket firings and give tours.

Ambitious travelers can hike the Grand Portage, the 8.5-mile trail that climbs from the post to the old site of Fort Charlotte on the Pigeon River. The portage enabled voyageurs and Indian travelers canoeing between Lake Superior and inland waterways to bypass the cataracts of the lower Pigeon River, including High Falls—at about 120 feet high, the tallest waterfall in Minnesota.

Yesterday's photo: Voyageur Press archives

FORT SNELLING

In 1825, Fort Snelling rose on a bluff at the confluence of the Minnesota and Mississippi rivers, a bulwark of early European American civilization, with Minnesota's first hospital, school, and library. In the decades that followed, the fort was the meeting place of Indians, traders, and ragtag settlers who later founded nearby St. Paul. During the Civil War, Union Army volunteers trained at the fort (as shown in this engraving from *Harper's Weekly*, 28 September 1861). The threat of highway construction in the 1950s spurred the U.S. Department of the Interior to designate the fort as the state's first National Historic Landmark. Nowadays, visitors to Historic Fort Snelling can watch period actors re-create a vivid picture of Minnesota in the late 1820s.

Yesterday's photo: Voyageur Press archives

Sod Homes

A pioneer family poses outside its "soddie," photographed in the early 1900s along the Minnesota–North Dakota border. As restless homesteaders ventured westward beyond the Mississippi, they left behind the woodlands and savannas for the wide-open prairies of western Minnesota and the Dakotas. These grasslands presented frontier settlers with rich soil but few materials to build a house. Where they could, homesteaders scrounged lumber from river bottoms. Where even this wood was scarce, pioneers found building material in the thick prairie sod. They cut sod of various lengths, roughly 4 inches thick and up to 2 feet wide. They stacked these chunks as they would bricks to form the walls. "The walls had now risen breast-high," Ole Rölvaag writes of a "soddie" in *Giants in the Earth*. "In its half-finished condition, the structure resembled more a bulwark against some enemy than anything intended to be a human habitation." Builders often dug their floor as deep as 4 feet to gain greater headroom without the walls becoming unstable. Branches were laid across the top of the walls and covered with a mat of straw and then more sod. Inside, the walls were smoothed with an ax, coated with mud, and then whitewashed. Floors were often packed earth. The only lumber used in the house's construction framed the door and the windows and formed the door itself. The finished house was well insulated in winter and stayed cool in summer, though it could be damp.

The Sod House on the Prairie, a bed and breakfast near Sanborn in southwestern Minnesota, provides an unusual opportunity to relive days on the frontier. Guests spend the night in a replica of an 1880s soddie, with a wood floor and six windows. They can also tour the "poor man's dugout," more typical of pioneer accommodations. With a dirt floor, few windows, and walls that bristle with dried roots and grass, the poor man's dugout was the kind of house pioneers "were glad to get out of and put behind them," says owner Virginia McCone.

Yesterday's photo: Voyageur Press archives

FARMERS AND FARMING

A man stands in a field of grain in the early 1900s. Wheat was a mainstay of early Minnesota farmers, and the flour-milling industry built the city of Minneapolis, which grew around the waterpower of St. Anthony Falls. In fact, Minnesota was once known as the wheat state.

By the time Minnesota was admitted to the union in 1858, treaties had been signed with Indians to open the land to settlement. The Homestead Act of 1862 promised 160 acres free to anyone who would live on the land and farm it for five years. Settlers streamed to the new state from central and northern Europe, especially Sweden, Norway, and Germany. (Despite its reputation as a land of Swedes, Minnesota has more Germans than any other ethnic group.) Immigrants were in the hunt for land, religious and social freedom, and lower taxes.

Most good farmland was settled by the late 1800s. A pamphlet published by the State Board of Immigration in 1913 promoted homesteading of "cut-over" and "logged-off" lands in northern Minnesota. Much of the land still available was swampy, but on some "the soil is rich and will grow large crops of small grain, vegetables, and hay. . . . The State of Minnesota now offers splendid

HOMESTEAD LANDS IN MINNESOTA

"THE FROST IS ON THE PUMPKIN
THE FODDER IN THE SHOCK."

ISSUED BY
STATE BOARD OF IMMIGRATION
ST. PAUL, MINN.

ADOLPH O. EBERHART,
Governor
A. D. STEPHENS,
Crookston, Minn.

JULIUS A. SCHMAHL,
Secretary of State.
J. A. NICHOLS,
Minnea olis, Minn.

S. G. IVERSON,
State Auditor.
FRED D. SHERMAN,
Commissioner of Immigration

opportunities for men of limited means to secure land and homes." Any U.S. citizen or person who had declared his intention to become a citizen, over twenty-one years of age, except married women, could buy land on forty-year's time with 15 percent down.

With mechanization and rising standards of living, farms today support fewer people than they once did. Migration to suburban areas causes residential development to spread, driving up land prices and property taxes. Nonetheless, farmers persist. Near Cologne, on the southwestern fringe of the Twin Cities, farmer Brian Buesjens continues to grow wheat.

Yesterday's photos: Minnesota Historical Society; Voyageur Press archives

Farm Life

Farmers pitched in to help their Blue Earth County neighbors with threshing chores in the 1890s. During the following century, tractors, self-powered combines, and other machinery took the place of cooperative farm work. So did the rising use of migrant labor. Since the early 1900s, itinerant workers have traveled to Minnesota to work in fields and canning factories. Today, each year roughly 20,000 seasonal workers, most of whom are Mexican American, come to the state, primarily from Texas. Despite a frost-free season ranging from just 100 days in the north to 150 days in the south, Minnesota's 79,000 farms, such as this farm near St. Charles, grow more sugar beets, oats, and green peas than farms in any other state. Minnesota ranks near the top in sweet corn, turkeys, hogs, cheese, wild rice, corn, soybeans, and spring wheat.

Yesterday's photo: Voyageur Press archives

LOGGING

Lumberjacks of the Rail Prairie Timber Camp stand proudly by the fruits of their day's work in the woods of central Minnesota in the winter of 1883–1884. The horses will pull the sled to the nearby Crow Wing River, where the logs will be piled on the riverbank until high water in spring will carry them to a sawmill downstream.

Some Minnesota loggers were local boys, others were immigrants, and still others were experienced woodcutters from Maine and Michigan, where they had already made neat work of felling the old-growth forest. Minnesota's logging industry began in the late 1830s in the St. Croix and Rum river valleys. Soon after, lumberjacks moved into the forests of central and northern Minnesota. By 1900, more than 40,000 loggers worked the woods, and Minnesota cut more timber than any other state.

Most prized were old-growth white pine, up to 4 feet across and more than 100 feet tall. In 1912, Frank Stenlund, an employee of the David Tozer Company's sawmill in south Stillwater, stood alongside two record-breaking boards, measuring 3 feet wide and 2.5 inches thick.

Many seemed to believe the forests were inexhaustible. "Centuries will hardly exhaust the pineries above us," James Madison Goodhue, editor of the *Minnesota Pioneer*, wrote in 1852. But the big logs of the Rum and St. Croix river valleys virtually disappeared by 1900. Old-growth forest elsewhere didn't last much longer. Few were alarmed at the rapid depletion of the state's timber. Indeed, settlers seemed eager to rid the state of trees, to make room for the farms that would follow. Typical was publisher Horace Greeley's remark in 1865: "This region will breathe freer when its last pine log is cut, run, sawed, rafted, and sold."

Today, loggers cut planted pines that have reached maturity. Hardwoods such as oak and maple provide high-quality lumber. But most logging focuses on pulpwood for paper—lower-value species such as aspen, jack pine, and balsam fir, such as the bolts in the photo that are being unloaded from a truck in Grand Marais.

Yesterday's photos: Minnesota Historical Society

PAUL BUNYAN

The legend of giant lumberjack Paul Bunyan is recounted in a 1940 postcard. "When Paul's pipe was going good, the clouds of smoke looked like a forest fire," reads one caption. The legend of Paul Bunyan may have grown from stories that circulated among lumberjacks working the north woods in the late 1800s. The first published story of Paul appeared in the *Detroit News* in 1910. James MacGillivray wrote a version of a tale he heard in a Michigan logging camp. In MacGillivray's "The Round River Drive," Paul and his men float logs to mill only to realize, as the riverbanks begin to look familiar, that the stream flows in a circle.

In 1914, William B. Laughead wrote and illustrated for the Red River Lumber Co. *Introducing Mr. Paul Bunyan of Westwood, California.* (The firm, based in Minneapolis, had moved many operations to the West Coast, perhaps explaining the book's odd title.) Laughead's tales were based on stories he'd heard in a logging camp

near Bemidji. To Laughead goes credit for introducing Babe the Blue Ox and Johnny Inkslinger, the camp clerk with an ink hose connected to his pen.

The Paul Bunyan legend has inspired several roadside attractions, including two concrete and steel statues of Paul and Babe on the shore of Lake Bemidji (shown in a 1938 postcard, which claims Paul "cut down six sections of timber with one stroke of his axe"). A giant Paul (26 feet tall as he sits!) greets children visiting This Old Farm Pioneer Village near Brainerd. The historic water tower in Brainerd is said to be Paul's flashlight or his knife handle. The red-and-white water tower in Pequot Lakes is Paul's fishing bobber. His cradle is found in Akeley, and his grave in Kelliher ("Paul Bunyan, born 1794, died 1899; Here lies Paul, and that's all").

Yesterday's photos: Voyageur Press archives

STATE CAPITOL

In 1871, Minnesota's first state capitol stood on Tenth and Cedar streets in a modest neighborhood of homes and churches overlooking the Mississippi. Built in 1853, when Minnesota was a territory, the first capitol burned during a legislative session in 1881. A second capitol was built on the same site within two years. But the red-brick Victorian building was doomed from the start, too cramped for its purposes even as it opened. (The second capitol continued to be used as a public building until it was torn down in 1937.)

In 1893, the legislature approved construction of a new capitol. Two years later, thirty-six-year-old Cass Gilbert was picked in a competition to be the architect. After spending some of his early career in New York, Gilbert designed many buildings in Minnesota. In all, he worked fifty years in the state. Among the buildings Gilbert designed in his career are the capitol buildings in Arkansas and West Virginia; the U.S. Supreme Court in Washington, D.C.; and the Woolworth Building in New York City.

Construction on the Minnesota State Capitol began in 1896; the building was opened to the public in 1905. Gilbert modeled the building on the U.S. Capitol and classic Italian and Greek buildings. His inspiration for the dome, which reaches 223 feet above the ground, was Michelangelo's dome for St. Peter's Basilica in Rome. The Minnesota capitol features European marble, native granite, limestone, and sandstone. Interior details include carvings, sculptures, and paintings of native and domestic animals and plants, such as loons and showy lady's-slippers. A golden chariot and four horses (the quadriga known as the "Progress of the State") sit at the base of the dome, overlooking the long stairway to the main entrance.

In an undated postcard, a densely constructed downtown sits between the capital approach and the Mississippi. A modern photo shows the capitol grounds. Cass Gilbert originally intended an uninterrupted landscaped mall sloping from the capitol to downtown. But over the years, roads have crisscrossed the mall. Some have been removed, but the construction of I-94 divided the land between the capitol, downtown, and the St. Paul Cathedral, carving up Gilbert's vision for a unified landscape.

Yesterday's photos: Minnesota Historical Society; Voyageur Press archives

BIRDS-EYE VIEW, ST. PAUL, MINN.

No. 139. V. O. Hammon Pub. Co., Minneapolis and Chicago

J. J. HILL'S RESIDENCE,   ST. PAUL, MINN.

James J. Hill Mansion

James J. Hill contracted the building of his home on Summit Avenue in 1891. Richardsonian Romanesque grandeur suited Hill, who also built the Great Northern Railway and who became one of the wealthiest figures of the Gilded Age. The Canadian-born Hill began his career as a shipping clerk on the St. Paul waterfront. By the time he died in 1916, he had amassed a fortune worth $63 million. He attributed his success to "work, hard work, intelligent work, and then more work." When complete, his home was the largest and most expensive in the state. The five floors included thirteen bathrooms, twenty-two fireplaces, sixteen crystal chandeliers, a 100-foot reception hall, and finely carved oak and mahogany trim. Today the James J. Hill House is open for tours, educational programs, concerts, lectures, and art exhibits.

Yesterday's photos: Minnesota Historical Society; Voyageur Press archives

Yesterday's photos: Minneapolis Public Library

EXCURSION BOATS, FOOT OF JACKSON STREET, ST. PAUL, MINN.

ST. PAUL RIVERFRONT

Paddle wheelers tie up at the St. Paul waterfront about 1905. From its inception, the city was a nexus of transportation, by simple virtue of topography and geography. It was the farthest upstream that large boats could ascend the Mississippi and unload cargo. Farther upstream lay 15 miles of rapids, shoals, and steep cliffs, and then St. Anthony Falls. As steamboat trade on the Mississippi grew, so did the settlement of St. Paul. The Galena Packet Company started weekly trips in 1847. St. Paul became the busiest port in the area. During a typical day in the 1850s, as many as two-dozen steamboats vied for dockage at the city's lower landing. Carriages and carts crowded the streets leading to the waterfront. Livestock bellowed. Stevedores shouted orders. Passengers debarked and boarded ships.

Today, barge, rail, and truck routes intersect at the St. Paul waterfront. At peak capacity, nearly 16 million tons of cargo passes through the St. Paul harbor. Grain, oilseeds, fertilizers, and scrap steel and aluminum ship downriver. Upriver come phosphates, fertilizers, salt, gravel, cement, asphalt, and coal.

Barge transport is one of the most fuel-efficient methods of hauling. A single "tow" containing fifteen barges pushed by a single towboat can carry the same tonnage of cargo as 225 railcars or 870 semitrailer trucks. A gallon of fuel can propel a ton of cargo 59 miles by truck, 202 miles by rail, and 514 miles by barge.

Paddle wheelers still call on St. Paul. The boats of the Delta Queen Steamboat Company, some of the largest ever to ply the river, occasionally pull into town.

St. Paul Skyline

St. Paul borders 17 miles of the Mississippi River, more than any other city. By 1905, transportation and industry transformed the waterfront to a bleak, uninviting, and inaccessible shore. But even then, Harriet Island (foreground) provided a recreational respite for St. Paul's citizens. Public Health Commissioner Justus Ohage purchased the 40-acre wooded island—named for pioneer schoolteacher Harriet Bishop—and transformed it at his own expense into a park. He donated it to the city in 1900. Contributions, including penny donations from city schoolkids, paid for the development of swimming beaches, day-care facilities, bathhouses, playgrounds, a bandstand, and a city zoo.

Worsening river pollution forced the bathhouses to close in the 1920s. In about 1950, the narrow channel between the island and the southern shore of the river was filled, so that Harriet Island was part of shore.

Recently, Harriet Island Regional Park was renovated to make it a more inviting gathering place. A public dock and a 20-foot-wide river walk that follows the shore provide access to the river. A pedestrian gateway through the levee at Water Street provides access to West Side residents. Crowds attending celebrations at Target Stage can spill out across Ohage Great Lawn. The renovated Clarence W. Wigington Pavilion also accommodates large groups.

Renovation to make Harriet Island more inviting is just part of a much larger effort to reconnect downtown St. Paul with the river that gave it life. New developments include plans for public parkways and housing along the Mississippi waterfront.

Yesterday's photo: Minneapolis Public Library

SUMMIT AVENUE

Newfangled automobiles navigate a nearly empty Summit Avenue in St. Paul in 1916. Summit gained its reputation for fashionableness not long after 1855, when Edward Duffield Neill, pastor of House of Hope Presbyterian Church, built his limestone home by the muddy trail that ran along the crest of the river bluff. With a lofty view of the valley, Summit Avenue soon became the scene of social one-upmanship. The wealthy of the Gilded Age built their homes along the road, which stretched from the Cathedral of St. Paul west to the Mississippi River gorge. Surreys and high-stepping trotters gave way to automobiles, but Summit remained the place to see and be seen. Neill's house couldn't keep up the pace; it was razed to make room for the mansion of St. Paul's king of the Gilded Age, James J. Hill.

A private home at 312 Summit, built in 1858, is the oldest house still standing along the street. The Italianate Livingston-Burbank-Griggs villa at 432 Summit, built in 1862, is one of the most striking Summit Avenue homes. Nobel Prize–winning author Sinclair Lewis lived briefly at 516 Summit. In summer 1919, as he rewrote *This Side of Paradise*, twenty-two-year-old F. Scott Fitzgerald rented an apartment in the brownstone row house at 599 Summit. Just east of Lexington Avenue is the three-story English Tudor Governor's Residence, built as a private home in 1910 and donated to the state in 1965.

During the mid-twentieth century, Summit Avenue fell into decline. Homes were split into apartments and fell into disrepair. "During the postwar decades, Summit Avenue was in great danger of disappearing, as have so many other fashionable boulevards when their moment of glory has passed," wrote historian Ernest R. Sandeen. But in the last several decades the avenue has revived. The eastern end of the avenue, with the oldest homes, was designated a historic district in the 1970s. In the 1990s, the remaining portion of the avenue was also so designated, securing Summit's future as a grand Victorian boulevard, looking much as it has for a century.

Yesterday's photo: Minnesota Historical Society

THE CATHEDRAL OF ST. PAUL

The Cathedral of St. Paul, shown in an undated illustration, stands at the east end of Summit Avenue, providing a religious counterweight to the similarly domed Minnesota State Capitol to the northeast.

The cathedral sprung from the vision of Archbishop John Ireland, and was designed by French architect Emmanuel Masqueray. Construction began in 1906. The cathedral was clad with St. Cloud granite. Many kinds of imported marble covered the columns and chapels surrounding the sanctuary. The building's copper dome soars to more than 300 feet, and like the dome of the capitol across the way, it suggests Michelangelo's St. Peter's Cathedral in Rome. The interior can seat 3,000 people. The first services were held in the cathedral in 1915. But neither Ireland nor Masqueray lived to see the building's interior completed in 1953.

Six of the cathedral's chapels are named for patron saints of ethnic groups that settled St. Paul: St. Anthony for Italians; St. John the Baptist for French Canadians; St. Patrick for Irish; St. Boniface for Germans; and Saints Cyril and Methodius for Slavs. The chapel of St. Therese of Lisieux is dedicated to missionaries.

The Archdiocese of St. Paul now covers twelve counties with more than 200 parishes and is home to more than 750,000 Catholics, such as the members of the wedding party shown in this photo. Nowadays, the cathedral shares its perch overlooking downtown St. Paul with the Minnesota History Center, completed in 1992.

Yesterday's photo: Voyageur Press archives

ST. PAUL CATHEDRAL

LANDMARK CENTER

The Richardsonian Romanesque Landmark Center, shown here in about 1915, started life in 1902 as the Federal Courts Building and Post Office for the upper Midwest. Its halls held the trials of many Prohibition-era thugs, including Ma Barker, Alvin "Creepy" Karpis, Lester "Babyface Nelson" Gillis, George "Machine Gun" Kelly, and John Dillinger. In 1967, the building was turned into federal offices, and before long it was scheduled for demolition.

In 1972, the federal government donated the building to the city. The louver-paneled ceiling, catwalks, green-painted walls, and wooden floors of the post office were torn out to reveal a four-story indoor courtyard with marble walls and floors. Several courtrooms were refurbished to provide luxurious space for receptions and dinners. In 1978, the Landmark reopened to the public. Today, it is owned and operated by Ramsey County as a center for the arts and for special events. It houses many nonprofit arts organizations, including the Ramsey County Historical Society and the Schubert Club Musical Instrument Museum, which maintains a collection of keyboards, phonographs, and instruments dating to the 1600s.

The Landmark Center faces Rice Park, established as a public square in 1849 and today one of the most attractive locations in the

city. Across the park from the Landmark sits the St. Paul Public Library. On one side is the Ordway Center for the Performing Arts; and on the other, the Saint Paul Hotel.

Yesterday's photos: Minneapolis Public Library; Voyageur Press archives

MICKEY'S DINER

Not much has changed inside Mickey's Diner since 1939, when the dining car was shipped by rail from its New Jersey factory and opened its doors in downtown St. Paul. It was designed and built by Jerry O'Mahoney Co. of Elizabeth, New Jersey, which sold many prefabricated diners during the first half of the twentieth century. Several O'Mahoney diners survive, mostly out east. Mickey's was the first designated to the National Register of Historic Places, in 1983. The design of the typical diner, including Mickey's, was inspired by fashionable railroad dining cars of the time. Mickey's is trimmed with a façade of yellow and red porcelain steel panels, a band of windows, and an art-deco neon sign. A glass vestibule was added to block wintry winds.

Since it opened, Mickey's has operated round the clock. Other than the capitol, Mickey's is perhaps the single most identifiable landmark in St. Paul. Mary Kiritschenko (in foreground) has worked at Mickey's for thirty-four years; Kaylynn Davis, for twelve; and Bert Mattson, the owner's son, has been hanging around since he was a kid.

Yesterday's photo: Minnesota Historical Society

WABASHA STREET

In 1915 in St. Paul, Wabasha Street was a flurry of activity. The thoroughfare developed as one of the major streets joining the Minnesota State Capitol grounds with downtown, and then across the Mississippi to the commercial and residential neighborhoods south of the river (on the so-called West Side—such is geography in St. Paul).

In the 1850s, residents of nascent St. Paul crossed the Mississippi River aboard a ferry. The Territorial Legislature in 1854 created the Saint Paul Bridge Co., which was assigned the task of building the area's first bridge across the river. The crossing, completed in 1859, was the first of several structures spanning the river at Wabasha Street. The name of the street derived from *Wapashaw* (spelled in various ways), the name of three successive generations of hereditary leaders of Dakota along the Mississippi River.

Today, Wabasha Street remains a vital commercial thoroughfare through downtown St. Paul. On the West Side are the famous Wabasha Caves, excavated for silica 150 years ago, later used to

grow mushrooms and for storage, and then used as a speakeasy during Prohibition. A nightclub for private events still occupies one cave.

Yesterday's photo: Minneapolis Public Library

as in parts of Wisconsin, Iowa, and South Dakota. At night, its signal reaches twenty-eight states and three Canadian provinces. One former WCCO announcer said he picked up the signal when he was stationed on Guadalcanal in the Pacific. Once a mainstay of rural audiences, WCCO dropped its well-known farm report in 2004. The station recently lost its top rating to KQRS-FM.

Today, the most recognized radio personality from Minnesota is undoubtedly Garrison Keillor, host of the live program *A Prairie Home Companion*. Keillor started *Prairie Home Companion*, named for a cemetery in Moorhead, as a morning broadcast on Minnesota Pubic Radio. He hosted the first live broadcast of the show with musical guests and fictional commercials in 1974. In 1978, the show moved to the then newly renovated World Theater (since renamed the Fitzgerald Theater) in St. Paul, which has served as the program's home base ever since. These days, more than 4 million people listen to *A Prairie Home Companion*, which is broadcast on over 500 public radio stations nationwide.

Yesterday's photo: Voyageur Press archives

MINNESOTA RADIO

A brochure from the late 1930s introduces fans of the still-new medium of radio to its national stars, including Jack Benny, Mary Livingstone, Dick Powell, Guy Lombardo, George Burns, and Gracie Allen. Radio opened a new world to rural families. Early radios were powered by stacks of batteries; the arrival of electricity made listening to the radio as easy as plugging it into the wall socket and turning a dial.

Minnesota's first radio station, WLB at the University of Minnesota, started broadcasting in 1921. By the end of the following year, nine radio stations were broadcasting in the Twin Cities, including WLAG, which was soon dubbed WCCO for Washburn Crosby Co., after the flour-milling company bought the station in 1924. WCCO soon became the most powerful radio station in the region and dominated the state's airwaves for well over a half century. The station gained a clear-channel license in 1929 so it could boost power to 50,000 watts. CBS added WCCO to its network in 1937. Just before World War II, the station changed frequency from 710 kHz to its present frequency of 830 kHz. During the day, the station can be picked up in most of Minnesota, as well

ICE PALACE

Ice Palace, St. Paul, Minn.

palace constructed of blocks of ice from Minnesota lakes was the centerpiece of St. Paul's first Winter Carnival in 1886. The new celebration was designed to rehabilitate the city's image after a New York reporter wrote that Saint Paul was "another Siberia, unfit for human habitation." Ice palaces became a tradition; another palace was constructed in 1887, and in 1888 an even-larger palace was built. Reaching 130 feet, it was the tallest building in the city. The first three castles were illuminated by then-new electric lights.

Over time, Winter Carnival ice palaces have been the exception rather than the rule. They appeared in 1937, 1939, 1941, and 1986. In 1992, the tallest ice palace yet took shape along the banks of the Mississippi on Harriet Island. It had twelve towers, the tallest reaching 150 feet. It was constructed from more than 25,000 blocks of ice harvested from Green Lake, west of the Twin Cities, which was chosen because of its clear water. The 2004 ice palace was the first built since 1992, and it was the first ice palace since 1941 that carnival-goers could actually enter and walk through.

The Winter Carnival is staged each January, with a treasure hunt for the carnival medallion; the selection of royalty; and a parade in often-freezing temperatures. At the heart of the celebration is a morality play: Virtuous King Boreas and his honor guard battle villainous Vulcans to defend winter in the city of St. Paul. Every year the good guys lose, and frigid weather gives way to thawing temperatures and eventual spring. Only Minnesotans would celebrate a battle to prevent the return of warm weather. Or perhaps they anticipated the threat of global warming.

Yesterday's photos: Minnesota Historical Society; Voyageur Press archives

WINTER ACTIVITIES

A homemade prototype of a snowmobile cruises over the frozen Mississippi River to Hastings in about 1910. Various designs for snow coaches and other vehicles sprung into being to provide practical transportation during Minnesota's frigid, snowy winters, and perhaps to also provide a diversion from the prolonged agony of the cold. Long coats and fur caps were the norm. While such outfits served well around town, they were hardly the most comfortable or effective clothing for vigorous winter activities.

Blustery weather could strike unexpectedly. The Armistice Day blizzard of 1940 followed a period of balmy November weather, catching motorists and hunters unaware. By the time the storm subsided on November 12, more than 2 feet of snow had fallen in central Minnesota, a 20-foot snow drift had formed near Willmar, and forty-nine Minnesotans had died.

Today, Minnesotans have the advantage of better forecasts, better clothes, and better snowmobiles—should they choose to use them. Musher Arleigh Jorgenson prefers to rely on his dogs to pull his sled through the winter wonderland of the Banadad Trail in northeastern Minnesota. Winter-lovers celebrate the cold weather at the annual Eelpout Festival on Leech Lake near Walker.

And even though winter can make driving (and parking) difficult, Minnesotans travel far and wide to compete in the odd but traditional game of curling, a combination of bowling, shuffleboard, and bocce ball. In the photo, Nick Meyers, sporting a Scottish kilt, plays in the mixed bonspiel at Mapleton's Curling Club.

Yesterday's photos: Minneapolis Star Journal*, Minnesota Historical Society*

St. Paul Streets

Yesterday's photo: Minneapolis Public Library

Automobiles were still a rarity on the streets of St. Paul in 1905, but streetcars, pedestrians, and horse-drawn carts hurried about on West Seventh Street. Seventh Street, originally called Fort Road because it joined downtown St. Paul to Fort Snelling, was an early commercial artery that ran through one of the city's first settlements. Fur traders and discharged soldiers settled the river bluff in the 1830s. Steamboats visited Upper Landing near present-day Chestnut Street during the mid-1800s. Irvine Park developed as a fashionable residential area beginning in 1849. During the late 1800s, immigrants flocked to the West Seventh Street neighborhood to work in the neighborhood factories, foundries, railroads, and breweries. German, Italian, Polish, Slavic, and Irish brogue filled the streets and shops. Horse-drawn streetcars began operation in 1872. The line was electrified in 1890.

In downtown St. Paul, times have changed but a few landmarks of the past remain.

PORKY'S DRIVE-IN

Souped-up cars tooled through Porky's Drive-In on St. Paul's University Avenue during the hot-rod and muscle-car era of the 1950s and 1960s. Drive-ins were the hang-out of the times, and perhaps none in the Twin Cities was busier than Porky's. Ray Truelson opened this legendary spot to see and be seen on University Avenue in St. Paul. It was followed by three drive-ins in Minneapolis—two on opposite ends of Lake Street and one on Lyndale. Truelson's son once explained that his father chose to cover his businesses with garish checkers to force motorists to take notice.

Drive-ins died as the muscle car faded. Truelson closed his Porky's, including the University Avenue drive-in, in 1979. It remained shuttered through the 1980s. The city then delivered an ultimatum: renovate or demolish. Porky's reopened in 1990, looking much as it had in its glory years. On summer nights, classic cars and hot rods once again stream through the parking lot, in tribute to the golden era of the muscle car.

Yesterday's photo: Minnesota Historical Society

Good corn makes good Hogs.
Copyright 1909 by Martin Post Card Co.

Copyrighted Photograph 1909 by Wm. H. Martin.

A load of extra good Apples

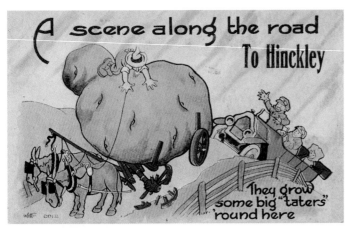

A scene along the road
To Hinckley

They grow
some big "taters"
'round here

A Pumpkin of Powerful growth.

A scene along the road
To Hinckley

Pulling beets

Pumpkins grown on our soil
are profitable

Harvesting a profitable crop of Onions.
Copyright 1909 by W. H. Martin.

FARMERS' MARKETS

ostcards of 1908–1909 boasted of stupendous crops and growing conditions. Fruits and vegetables of more normal proportions were in great demand in the growing cities of St. Paul and Minneapolis. Beginning in 1853 in St. Paul and 1876 in Minneapolis, farmers from all around began hauling produce to city farmers' markets, first to sell to small grocers and then directly to consumers. The tradition continues unabated.

In St. Paul, about 200 local growers and producers bring their products to the market in Lowertown, including vegetables, fruits, cut flowers, and honey. The market is open Friday afternoons and weekend mornings. More than $2 million in recent improvements have made the market more convenient and comfortable for producers and shoppers, who sometimes exceed 25,000 during peak season. A winter market sells honey, eggs, and dairy products.

In Minneapolis, more than 200 vendors sell products at the main market on Lyndale Avenue. The market has expanded to include a satellite on the Nicollet Mall, allowing downtown workers and residents access to the freshest produce, in the shadows of Minnesota's tallest buildings.

Yesterday's photos: Voyageur Press archives

MINNESOTA BARNS

In this photo from about 1900, neighbors pitch in to help raise a barn on a dairy farm near the Rainy River in far northern Minnesota. In those days, people set aside work on their own farms to help a neighbor in need. Workers took no pay except for a hearty lunch in the field and the assurance that others would return the favor when the need arose.

Barns varied from region to region, depending on age, purpose built, available materials, and the builders' ethnic heritage. People had their own way of doing things that nonetheless reflected the knowledge and habits of their neighbors. The barns that resulted from community collaborations were testaments to the times and to the close-knittedness of rural communities.

What goes up, must come down. In the photo, taken in Belle Plaine, a century-old barn has outlived its usefulness and is now being disassembled for its valuable old-growth wood, the likes of which is hard to find these days. The lumber was so valuable it was bundled up and trucked to New Mexico for a cabin.

Some old barns are valuable as living relics. Four miles from Red Wing, the pictured round dairy barn, built by Henry and Mary Dammon in 1914, has been converted to a cozy bed and breakfast.

Yesterday's photo: Minnesota Historical Society

TRACTOR CREWS

A crew poses with a steam-powered threshing machine in 1922. Ever since the J. I. Case Co. of Racine, Wisconsin, produced what it claimed was the first steam engine for farm use in 1869, steam power began taking farmwork away from such draft-horse breeds as Belgians and Percherons.

But steam-powered machinery was heavy, bulky, and not adaptable. In 1892, Case introduced its first gas engine for farmers, who immediately liked these smaller, more versatile gas "traction engines." In 1917, Fordson produced the first mass-produced tractor, and in 1918, a farm-implement manufacturer named John Deere bought the maker of Waterloo Boy tractors. The introduction of power take-off meant that mobile tractors could power machines such as binders and mowers. In 1924, International Harvester introduced the tricycle-style tractor, with front wheels close together for cultivating row crops. Allis-Chalmers introduced rubber tires in 1932.

When the young couple in the photo tried out the latest John Deere models on display at the Minnesota State Fair's Machinery Hill in the 1930s, the Deere Model A and the smaller Model B were becoming established as the most popular models in the Deere line. Known as "Johnny Poppers" for their distinctive two-cylinder-engine sound, the bright green tractors were emblematic of Minnesota farms. Kids at play imagined riding their own tractor.

As American farms grew larger, the farm labor force shrunk and machinery grew ever more prevalent. During the 1930s, the number of tractors at work on American farms doubled to some 1.6 million. Workhorses had been put out to pasture, literally and figuratively.

By 1974, the average Minnesota farm had 2.6 tractors and no workhorses. Unlike their fathers or grandfathers, farmers such as Tom (left) and Phil Jacobs of Bird Island no longer hitch a horse to their plow or other equipment.

Yesterday's photos: Minnesota State Fair; John Runk, Minnesota Historical Society; Voyageur Press archives

FARMSTEADS

A family poses on their typical Minnesota farmstead in the 1950s. Since the "golden age" of farming ended with bankruptcies at the close of World War I, farm income declines, machinery replaced human and animal labor, farms grew larger, and rural residents increasingly moved to towns and cities. In 1940 in Minnesota, half the state's population still lived in small towns or rural areas. The rural

portion of the population dropped to 34 percent in 1970. After 1980, farm prices dropped precipitously, land values plunged, and farmers sunk further in to debt. The trend toward larger farms and fewer farmers continues.

In southwestern Minnesota, some landowners have opted to farm the wind. Nearly 500 turbines produce electricity from wind blowing across Buffalo Ridge, one of the windiest spots in the state, where wind blows an average of 17 miles per hour.

More than fifty wind projects in Minnesota operate nearly 700 turbines, to produce enough electricity to power more than 20,000 homes. Minnesota ranks fourth in the nation in installed wind capacity. About 70 percent of the state's wind-energy production is centered in six counties in southwestern Minnesota.

Farmers capitalize on their wind energy in various ways. Some lease their wind rights to a developer for up to $5,000 per turbine. Some form a joint venture. Others buy the turbines outright. In Lincoln County, landowners receive more than $500,000 a year for land leased or purchased by wind developers.

Yesterday's photo: Voyageur Press archives

MINNESOTA COWS

I n this undated photograph at right, a docile cow proves
that livestock is a Minnesota farmer's best friend. Cattle
have been a Minnesota fixture since 1823, when cattle
were driven from St. Louis along the Mississippi to Fort
Snelling. The herd was later augmented with cattle from the
Selkirk Colony in Manitoba. Minnesota's livestock industry began to grow in the 1860s, after treaties with the Dakota opened
lands in southern Minnesota to settlers. Early on, Shorthorns were
common, used mainly for milk and work. Older animals, unfit
for milk production or work, were slaughtered. In the late 1800s,

prominent Minnesotans, including James J. Hill, imported pure-bred cattle from Europe and the East Coast, to establish dairy- and beef-cattle herds.

Today, more than 15,000 Minnesota farms raise beef cattle and about 9,000 raise dairy cows, for a total of nearly 2.5 million cattle. Among counties, Stearns has the most cows, with more than 180,000 head. Cattle make up the largest segment of the state's animal industry. Minnesota ranks fifth among states in milk production, and seventh in production of red meat. Most cattle operations are family farms. About 85 percent have been in the family for more than twenty-five years.

Animal husbandry has been a staple of Minnesota higher education. In an undated photograph, top left University of Minnesota students learn bovine anatomy and milking techniques. In 1868, the university bought land in Minneapolis to establish an agricultural college and experimental farm. In 1882, 155 acres were purchased at the site of the present St. Paul campus for the School of Agriculture and Experiment Station. A two-year course included lectures and training in animal breeding, feeding, farm hygiene, and veterinary science.

Learning occurs at other venues as well. Cows are always a big hit at the Minnesota State Fair. Kids still learn how to milk, but nowadays with a fake cow. And young farmers-to-be still bring their prize beef and dairy animals to the fair for competition.

Yesterday's photos: Minnesota State Fair; Minneapolis Public Library

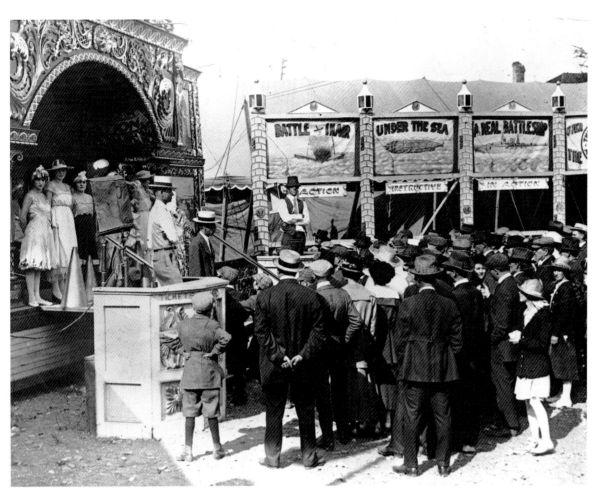

STATE FAIR MIDWAY

The grounds have been spiffed up a bit since the midway carnies packed up after the 1904 Minnesota State Fair midway show. Otherwise, much has remained the same in the Midway: freak shows, carnival barkers, games of chance. Did the smell of corn dogs drift on the air a century ago?

In 1917, during World War I, the Midway took on a martial air with exhibits on warplanes, submarines, and ships. Then, as today, the curious line up to pay money and take a peek.

The state fair is even older than the state itself, if that's possible. Four territorial fairs predated the admission of Minnesota to the union in 1858. The first *state* fair was held in 1859. Since then, the fair has been held every year except five: 1861 and 1862, because of the disruption of the Civil War and the Dakota Indian War in southwestern Minnesota; 1893, because of scheduling conflicts with the World's Columbian Exposition in Chicago; 1945, because of World War II fuel shortages; and 1946, because of a polio epidemic.

The location has also changed through the years. The first fair was held in what would later be downtown Minneapolis. Early on, the venue changed yearly from St. Paul, to Rochester, to Red Wing, to Winona, and to Owatonna. Civic boosters from St. Paul and Minneapolis, always eager to outdo their rivals, worked to win the fair for their own cities. In 1885, Ramsey County donated the site of the then county poor farm, midway between Minneapolis and St. Paul. The location has been home to the fair ever since.

Yesterday's photo: Minnesota Historical Society

State Fair Prizewinners

P roud competitors in the 1926 Minnesota State Fair pose with their prizewinning gladioluses, pies, breads, and carrots. The fair began when Minnesota was still a territory, with exhibitions and competitions in agriculture and home economics to promote farming and the skills of rural life. The farming theme has remained strong, even as the Minnesota economy has diversified. Today at the state fair, people compete in dairy products, bees and honey, Christmas trees, flowers, fruit, wine, potatoes, vegetables, giant pumpkins, dairy cattle, beef cattle, sheep, swine, English horses, workhorses, western horses, chickens, ducks, geese, turkeys, pigeons, rabbits, llamas, and tractor driving.

Over the years, the fair has beefed up its nonagricultural events, including Grandstand entertainment; technological, industrial and governmental exhibits (such as the popular fish pond by the Minnesota Department of Natural Resources); and of course, the ever-changing array of food booths. Animal and home-economics competition remains keen, as well, and the animal barns are popular venues for fairgoers. In the photo, competitors relax in the horse barn, while displaying awards for their blue-ribbon efforts.

Yesterday's photos: Minnesota Historical Society

Spiral Bridge, Hastings, Minn.

HASTINGS

The unique Hastings Spiral Bridge (shown in an undated postcard) answered two competing desires when it was built in 1895: the shipping industry's desire for a bridge with at least 55 feet of clearance over the Mississippi River, for boat traffic, and the desire of city fathers for a bridge that delivered traffic into the downtown rather than over and beyond it.

The town of Hastings had been platted in 1853, only a couple of years after a treaty with the Dakota allowed settlement of the region. The name *Hastings*, drawn from a hat, was the middle name of Henry Sibley, the first governor of Minnesota. A year after the town was platted, a rope ferry carried horses and riders across the river. The first settlers arrived by river. But as large as it was, the Mississippi wasn't always reliable for transportation. When water was low, steamboats could not reach St. Paul, the usual head of navigation, so had to stop instead at Hastings.

While the Mississippi River served as transportation, the Vermillion River, which joined the Mississippi at Hastings, provided waterpower for four flour mills. (The ruins of one mill, built by Alexander Ramsey in 1855, were designated a state historical site and are still viewable today.) Forty-two foot Vermillion Falls in Hastings is a reminder of the stream's potential for waterpower.

As horses gave way to automobiles and heavy trucks began to use the highways, the old Spiral Bridge was unable to support the load. It was demolished in 1951 and replaced with a more conventional span.

Today, about 20,000 people live in Hastings, many in outlying neighborhoods. But the downtown's old stone commercial buildings and Victorian homes provide a charming glimpse of a past life in one of Minnesota's oldest river towns.

Yesterday's photo: Voyageur Press archives

STREET SCENE, STILLWATER, MINN

STILLWATER

The car styles and the signs have changed, but the intersection of Main and Chestnut in downtown Stillwater otherwise looks much the same today as it did in a postcard from the 1940s. Stillwater, a picturesque town of 16,000 on the banks of the beautiful St. Croix River, proclaims itself the birthplace of Minnesota and takes pride in preserving its historic appearance.

Founded in 1843, Stillwater is one of the state's oldest towns. It was the site of the territorial convention in 1848, which led to the formation of the Minnesota Territory the following year. Through the remainder of the 1800s, Stillwater was one of the busiest sawmill towns in the state, as pine logs cut from forests to the north floated down the St. Croix to a logging "boom," a barrier of floating logs 2 miles above town. There, up to 600 men sorted logs by the owners' brands and sent them downstream to sawmills. Old photographs show the river to be a corduroy of logs. Shipments peaked in 1890, and then fell quickly; the boom folded in 1914. The following year, the *Ottumwa Belle* towed the last raft of lumber downstream.

Nowadays, tourists flood Stillwater streets in summer and fall. Craft shops, boutique malls, restaurants, bars, and antique shops occupy many of the town's old buildings. Visitors can tour the river valley aboard the *Minnesota Zephyr,* a dinner train that makes a short run along the St. Croix. Tourists can also see the area onboard the *Andiamo* showboat or onboard a replica of the trolleys that ran through town a century ago.

Yesterday's photo: Minnesota Historical Society

RIVERBOATS

The steamboat *Ben Hur* lands at the Stillwater levee in 1911, after an excursion from Red Wing up the Mississippi and St. Croix rivers. Built in Marietta, Georgia, in 1887, the 165-foot-long sternwheeler typified the packets operating on the Mississippi and its tributaries during the mid and late 1800s. Before the development of railroads, riverboats were the main mode of transportation to the territory that would become known as Minnesota. In the 1850s, settlers to the newly opened lands arrived at river towns such as Red Wing and Stillwater by boat. For a short time, the boats were the flamboyant royalty of the territory. But their end came quickly. Rails from Chicago reached the Mississippi in 1854. Rail transportation initially spurred the steamboat trade, but as tracks crossed and followed the major rivers, trains provided shippers and travelers a more reliable and faster alternative to riverboats. Though steamboats still carried passengers during the early 1900s, their days as a vital, practical form of transportation were finished by this time.

Today, replicas of old riverboats such as the *Taylors Falls Princess*—shown here navigating the swift water of the St.

Croix—take sightseers along the rivers that once formed a network of transportation across the upper Midwest. Tourism by riverboat in fact has a long history. As early as 1835, painter George Catlin took a trip he called a "fashionable tour" by riverboat to the upper Mississippi.

Yesterday's photo: John Runk, Minnesota Historical Society

NORTHFIELD AND THE
JAMES-YOUNGER GANG ROBBERY

Northfield was a growing town on the Cannon River when this photograph was taken in 1870. Just six years later, a gang that included Cole, Bob, and Jim Younger—who robbed banks with Frank and Jesse James across the Midwest and South—rode into town.

The gunmen wore dirty white dusters to hide their weapons. Two outlaws slipped inside the First National Bank on Division Street and demanded money. When clerk Joseph Lee Heywood refused to turn it over, they shot him dead. As townspeople realized the bank was being robbed, they began to shoot. A robber posted outside the bank jumped on his horse. The two men inside the bank also fled as shots rang out from the street and upper floor windows. Northfield resident Nicholas Gustavson, from Sweden, was killed. So were two gang members, Clell Miller (upper left) and Bill Chadwell (upper right).

Cole and Bob Younger (both wounded), Jim Younger, Charles Pitts, and possibly Frank and Jesse James rode out of town under heavy gunfire, with none of the bank's money But townsfolk didn't leave it at that; they organized posses to chase the robbers. As the manhunt grew, as many as 2,000 men chased the gang for weeks over a distance of 400 miles.

The Youngers were eventually captured in a gunfight near Madelia, Minnesota, where Charles Pitts (center left) was killed. Cole (center right), Jim (lower left), and Bob (lower right) Younger were tried in Faribault, convicted of murder, and sent to the state prison in Stillwater. Bob died in prison. Jim and Cole were pardoned in 1901. Jim committed suicide the following year, but Cole lived until 1916.

The failed raid, portrayed in many books and movies, is reenacted every September during the Defeat of Jesse James Days in Northfield. Riders in white dusters re-create the chaos as would-be townspeople fire on the gang. Thousands gather to see the spectacle, watch a parade, and stroll by arts and crafts exhibits.

Yesterday's photos: Minnesota Historical Society

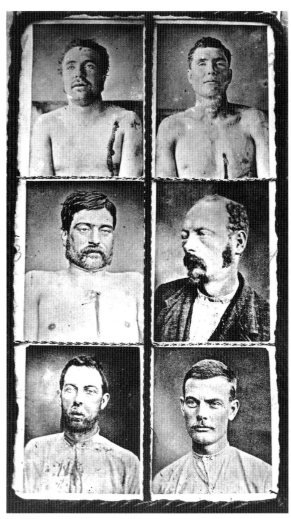

Mayo Clinic

The Mayo Clinic in Rochester, shown here in an undated postcard, sprang from the medical practice of William W. Mayo, who opened his Rochester office in 1863, and his sons, William J. and Charles H. The family was instrumental in building the St. Mary's Hospital in 1889. During the next several years, the Mayo brothers began using innovative and successful techniques in treatment, allowing doctors to better investigate patient illnesses and to get advice from other specialists. Their methods soon attracted international attention.

Today, more than 2,500 physicians and scientists and 42,000 allied health staff work at the Mayo Medical Center (a clinic and two affiliated hospitals), treating a half-million patients a year. Research at the clinic has included isolating cortisone for the treatment of arthritis; designing a mask and an anti-blackout suit for high-altitude test pilots; developing technology for open-heart surgery; advancing the use of lasers to destroy brain tumors; and using chemicals to dissolve gallstones without surgery. The clinic is made up of more than thirty buildings, including the nineteen-story Mayo Building.

Historian Helen Clapesattle Shugg has referred to the "paradox of Rochester"—that so much technological skill and such cosmopolitan sensibilities should be found in a "little river valley town in Midwestern America." Rochester, with about 86,000 people, is the commercial and industrial center of the region. With high-paying jobs and an educated and technologically skilled workforce (IBM is another larger employer in town), Rochester is often ranked among the nation's most livable cities.

Yesterday's photo: Voyageur Press archives

RED WING

In 1870, Red Wing's Main Street was just beginning to take shape, with the unmistakable outline of Barn Bluff rising in the background. Red Wing was named for Dakota chief Ta-tan-ka-mani (Walking Buffalo), who was also known as Red Wing, for the scarlet swan wing that served as talisman for his lineage. His band of Mdewakanton Dakotas lived near the present site of town.

One of Minnesota's earliest cities, Red Wing was settled by folks traveling up the Mississippi after treaties opened the area to settlement. Soon farms began to spread across the valleys on the west side of the river, and Red Wing became an important port for grain shipments to markets downstream. Briefly, Goodhue County farms produced more wheat than those of any other county in the country. Lumber barons, mill owners, and bankers built antebellum and Victorian monuments in the town.

The centerpiece of the historic downtown is the St. James Hotel on Main Street. Built in 1874, the St. James had fallen into despair. In 1977, the Red Wing Shoe Co. purchased and renovated it. Known for its hunting, hiking, and work boots, the company is a major employer in town, providing more than 700 jobs. The largest employer in town is Treasure Island Casino, owned by the Prairie Island Indian Community, many members of which are descendants of the site's original Mdewakanton Dakota inhabitants.

Yesterday's photo: Minnesota Historical Society

LANESBORO AND THE ROOT RIVER VALLEY

Founded after the Civil War in the steep valley of the South Branch of the Root River, Lanesboro has a story befitting Rip Van Winkle. By the 1920s, when this card was postmarked, loggers and farmers had cleared most of the forests and grasslands from the rugged limestone bluff country of southeastern Minnesota. Rain caused disastrous flooding. The town's fortunes dwindled, as though time passed it by. When the railroad along the river was abandoned in 1971, the rail bed was converted to the Root River State Trail. Lanesboro's fortunes revived as cyclists and hikers visited its restaurants and historic hotels by the thousands. Better conservation practices on bluff-land farms have helped stem the loss of land, and anglers fish for trout once again in the South Branch.

Yesterday's photo: Voyageur Press archives

THE IRON RANGE

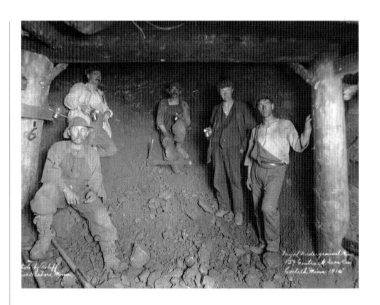

Miners in the Fayal underground iron mine near Eveleth pause in their work in 1919. With picks, shovels, and backbreaking labor, they excavated the rich natural ore that made the iron mines of northern Minnesota the most productive in the world.

Iron mining began in northern Minnesota with the opening of the Soudan underground mine near Tower, on the so-called Vermillion Range. The first trainload of commercial-grade ore was shipped in 1884. Townspeople gathered along the tracks and tossed chunks of ore into the cars as the train pulled out.

To the south lay a giant ore body, dubbed the Mesabi Range for the red giant of Anishinabe mythology. The deposit was 65 percent iron, and lay so near the surface that miners were able to excavate it with steam shovels, creating sprawling open-pit mines. Eventually miners discovered that the rich ore stretched 120 miles from Grand Rapids to Hoyt Lakes. The Mesabi has proved to be one of the biggest ore bodies in the world, yielding more than 3 billion tons of ore. Mesabi iron built the guns, tanks, and armament that won World War II. For years, Minnesota produced 25 percent of the world's iron ore. The Hull-Rust-Mahoning Mine near Hibbing grew to be the largest open-pit iron mine in the world.

During the mid-1900s, the richest ore played out. Miners began to take the lean ore known as taconite. Giant shovels dump the hard rock into trucks capable of carrying more than 200 tons—trucks whose tires dwarf their operators. At a nearby plant, the taconite is crushed, the ore is concentrated, and the concentrate is formed into pellets that are about 65 percent iron.

Many of the old open-pit mines have been abandoned. Some, now filled with water, have been stocked with fish and are popular recreation sites.

Yesterday's photos: Library of Congress; Minnesota Historical Society

THIRD AVE LOOKING NORTH HIBBING MINN. COPYRIHT 1910 BY B. BLOOM MPL.

HIBBING

Northern Minnesota's iron mines drew workers from more than forty nationalities, including Finns, Slovenes, Italians, Swedes, Croatians, Norwegians, English-speaking Canadians, Brits, Poles, Montenegrins, Germans, Serbs, and French Canadians. In 1910, in towns such as Hibbing, nearly half of the population was foreign-born. In rural areas, the percentage was even higher.

Hibbing was unusual among Iron Range towns in that it was once completely moved to make way for the expanding Hull-Rust-Mahoning open-pit mine. The town, named for prospector Frank Hibbing, was established in 1893. Two years later, the mine began shipping ore. Soon it was discovered the new town sat square over the ore body. During two years, beginning in 1919, 185 houses and twenty commercial buildings were hauled 2 miles south with horses, cables, and log rollers, at a rate of about 750 feet per hour. Some large buildings were cut in half. Christ Memorial Church was disassembled stone by stone, moved, and rebuilt. Steam shovels scooped up graves. The remains of North Hibbing, including signs, streetlights, and a few old foundations, now line a grid of streets. Interpretive displays tell of the buildings that once stood there and the relocation of the town.

Today, Hibbing, with a population of about 17,000, is the largest city on the Iron Range. The iron-mining workforce has dropped precipitously in the last thirty years, but the industry is still vital, supporting main-street businesses in Hibbing and other Iron Range communities.

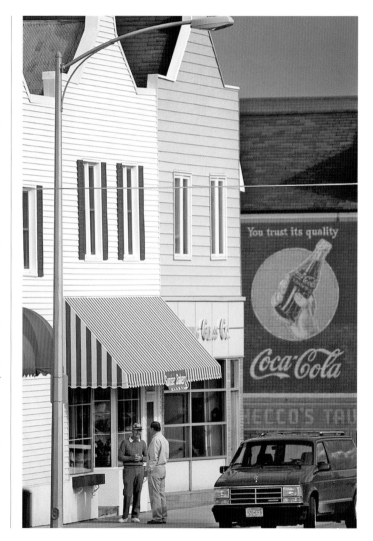

Yesterday's photo: Voyageur Press archives

LIGHTHOUSES

Split Rock Lighthouse is the most imposing and picturesque lighthouse on Lake Superior. Perhaps no other landmark on the North Shore—and perhaps in all of Minnesota—has been so often depicted in postcards and photographs.

The lighthouse was built after autumn storms in 1905 wrecked six boats and killed more than 200 sailors. Metallic deposits in the area deflected compass needles, making navigation along the shore treacherous. Since roads did not reach the promontory, derricks were built atop the 130-foot-high cliff to lift some 300 tons of building material from the decks of ships. After it entered service in 1910, the Split Rock Light served Lake Superior for sixty years. The scrupulously polished Fresnel lens that focused the beam of light over the lake floated on a bearing of 250 pounds of liquid mercury.

Split Rock Lighthouse

Decommissioned in 1960, Split Rock Lighthouse is now a state historic site. Visitors can climb the light tower, where the lens still rests. They also can tour the fog-signal building; residences for three lighthouse keepers and their families; and a history center with exhibits on shipping, shipwrecks, and commercial fishing and a film about the lighthouse. Every November 10, the beacon is lit in memory of the twenty-nine men who died when the iron-ore freighter *Edmund Fitzgerald* sank in 1975.

Some decommissioned Lake Superior lights, such as the Lighthouse Bed and Breakfast Inn near the Two Harbors ore docks, have found new life in private ownership. Others, however, have been torn down or are slowly falling into ruin.

Yesterday's photos: Minnesota Historical Society; Voyageur Press archives

NIGHT LIFE AT AERIAL LIFT, DULUTH, MINN.— 64

DULUTH AERIAL LIFT BRIDGE

Entering the harbor, an ore freighter passes beneath the Duluth Aerial Life Bridge, an emblematic landmark in Minnesota's city by the bay, portrayed on an undated postcard. A section of the bridge rises 138 feet to allow boats to pass underneath through the Duluth Ship Canal. The canal separates that mainland (and most of the city) from Minnesota Point, a long sand spit that protects the harbor. While the point is natural, the canal is not. The natural channel lies on the Wisconsin side of the sand spit. Residents of Superior, Wisconsin, eager to protect the natural advantage of having the ship canal on their side of the harbor, sought to go to court to prevent Duluth from digging its own entrance. But Duluth residents got wind of the plan and dug the channel in the night—even private citizens attacked the sand spit with shovels—to open the passage before Superior could prevail.

Cars cross the lift bridge on their way to Minnesota Point (known locally as Park Point), a casual beachside neighborhood and a pleasant place to hike, bike, or watch birds. Next to the lift bridge is the bustling neighborhood of Canal Park, with lofts, retails stores, and restaurants. In the Lake Superior Maritime Visitors Center, dedicated to Great Lakes shipping, you can tour a ship's pilothouse, engine room, and crew quarters; inspect models of Great Lakes boats; and see exhibits of shipwrecks. The museum provides a clear view of vessels, such as the oceangoing freighter (known as a "salty") in the photograph that is waiting its turn to enter the harbor beneath the Aerial Lift Bridge.

Yesterday's photo: Voyageur Press archives

DULUTH SKYLINE

Were San Francisco not several times larger and much more famous, Tony Bennett might have left his heart in Duluth—Minnesota's city by the bay. Few cities claim so beautiful a setting. *The WPA Guide to Minnesota* called Duluth "a Lilliputian village in a mammoth rock garden." The city, nestled at the western tip of Lake Superior, runs along the lake for 24 miles. "Because of the city's narrowness," says the guidebook, "the countryside seems always, in Duluth, to be crowding down to its very back doors."

The city was named for French explorer Daniel Greysolon, Sieur Duluth, who arrived in 1679. Trade and transportation with Anishinabe commenced immediately upon his arrival. The current town site, at the mouth of the St. Louis River, served as a gateway between the Great Lakes and the interior waterways of northern Minnesota and Canada.

Steep hillsides are characteristic of Duluth. The Incline Railway was built in the 1890s to carry passengers a half-mile uphill from Superior Street on Seventh Avenue West. Fire destroyed the railway in 1901; it was not rebuilt for a decade. The railway was dismantled in 1939.

Duluth continues to thrive as an international port, shipping taconite pellets to steel plants on the lower lakes, and grain and wood products to eastern U.S. and European ports.

Yesterday's photos: Voyageur Press archives

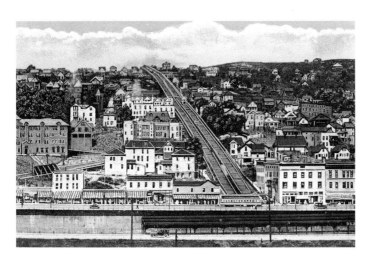

22   View from Top of Famous Incline Railway, Duluth, Minn.

LAKE SUPERIOR SHIPPING

A freighter glides into a slip in the Duluth harbor to take on a load of iron ore in this undated illustration below. Another freighter is docked to receive grain in an undated photograph left.

In 1855, with the construction of locks at Sault Ste. Marie at the east end of Lake Superior, large ships began to pass between Duluth and large cities elsewhere on the Great Lakes. In 1870, a railroad joined Duluth with St. Paul. Shipments of grain grown out west began to arrive in Duluth, for shipment to the East. Meanwhile, burgeoning iron mines in northern Minnesota shipped ore via Duluth to steel mills on the lower lakes, especially Lake Michigan. More recently, coal from western states has been a major cargo passing through Duluth.

Today, Duluth is the largest port on the Great Lakes and one of the largest inland seaports in the world, shipping products from the Midwest, Great Plains, and Canada's western provinces. The shoreline of the port stretches 49 miles, with 17 miles of dredged channels. On average, 40 million metric tons of cargo pass through Duluth and Superior (its Wisconsin counterpart across the bay) aboard 1,100 vessels each year. The port ranks fifth nationally in coal, and first in iron ore and grain (primarily wheat, corn, and soybeans). Many grain shipments head to European ports. The Duluth harbor lies 2,342 miles—less than a week by freighter—from the Atlantic.

Loading Iron Ore on Lake Superior

ORE BOATS ENTERING ORE DOCKS FOR CARGO

Yesterday's photos: Minneapolis Public Library; Voyageur Press archives

Typacle

COMMERCIAL FISHING

Boats rest at a small fishing village on the North Shore of Lake Superior in this undated illustration. During the early twentieth century, Anishinabe and Norwegian villages and homesteads dotted the North Shore. During open-water season, men from the settlements risked their lives to venture out on Superior to tend nets for lake trout, lake whitefish, and ciscoes (known also as tullibees or lake herring).

The days of commercial fishing were numbered. In retrospect, fishermen probably overharvested. More dramatically, the sea lamprey, native to the Atlantic, sneaked into the upper Great Lakes with the deepening of the Welland Canal in 1919, reaching Lake Superior in 1946. During the 1950s, the signs and effects of predatory lamprey became more and more evident. The harvest of lake trout, which were especially vulnerable, plunged. Commercial fishing for lake trout was limited to Indian tribes and a small "assessment" harvest by a few non-Indians.

Within years, many commercial fishermen bailed out of the business. Dick Eckel of Hovland and Tommy Eckel of Grand Marais are among the stalwart few who have continued to make a go of harvesting whitefish and ciscoes for local markets and restaurants.

Through intense stocking, and costly poisoning of sea lamprey in their spawning streams, lake trout have made a remarkable recovery—so much so that Minnesota is considering opening a limited commercial harvest.

Yesterday's photo: Voyageur Press archives

Main Street
Grand Marais, Minn

GRAND MARAIS

In this photo from 1935, the main street of Grand Marais is just beginning to show its promise as a popular tourist spot along the North Shore of Lake Superior. The town, originally an Anishinabe village, was located to take advantage of a large natural harbor. It has served as a fur-trading post, a fishing center, a lumber town, and eventually the site of a Coast Guard station. With the opening of a highway along the North Shore, Grand Marais found itself at a strategic juncture: the main route headed north to Grand Portage and then to the Canadian twin cities of Port Arthur and Fort William (now collectively know as Thunder Bay). Off to the west of Grand Marais is the Gunflint Trail, which leads to a series of beautiful, popular lakes for fishing, canoeing, and plain enjoyment.

Today, Grand Marais is more popular than ever, with restaurants, coffee shops, art galleries, and outfitters such as the Beaver House tackle shop. Traditional summertime activities such as fishing, canoeing, and sailing have been augmented by sea kayaking, mountain biking, photography, backpacking, and even moose watching. In winter, cross-country skiers flock to the area at the northeastern tip of Minnesota, to take advantage of some of the deepest snow in the state.

Yesterday's photo: Minnesota Historical Society; Voyageur Press archives

Another one just below this

Gooseberry Falls and River

GOOSEBERRY FALLS

Completion of Highway 61 along the North Shore in 1924 introduced tourists to the thundering cascades of rivers such as the Gooseberry, which plunged from the hills down to Lake Superior. Until that time, the shore had been the province of a few Anishinabe and Norwegian fishermen and their families. Boats brought mail and supplies during three seasons; dog sleds performed the chore in winter.

With the increase of travel along the shore, there was concern that the rich would buy up access to the area's scenic treasures. To protect public access to the shore's most beautiful places, the state began an ambitious campaign to expand its system of state parks. The legislature authorized the protection of the area around several falls of the Gooseberry River in 1933. Civilian Conservation Corps workers built the stone and log buildings that stand today. They also laid out the first campground, picnic area, and trails.

Today, 1,700-acre Gooseberry Falls State Park is one of the most popular state parks, visited by more than a half-million people each year, many of whom hike the trails to the thundering falls near the highway or linger in the new visitors' center. The cascading tributaries to Lake Superior form the backdrop of all the popular state parks along the shore, including Tettegouche, Manitou, Cascade, and Judge C. R. Magney. This system of parks provides a legacy of public access to the wild areas along Superior's rapidly developing coast.

Yesterday's photo: Voyageur Press archives

WOLVES

With ten wolf pelts draped across his horse, Ben Bendixon set out for the Roseau County auditor's office in January 1916 to collect his bounty.

Though the frightening appearance and woeful howl of wolves stir the soul, the animals have rarely lived up to their fearsome reputation. Nonetheless, they are frequently the bane of farmers, ranchers, and herdsmen. Once common throughout Minnesota, wolves were hunted, trapped, and poisoned, until they disappeared from everywhere but the relatively inaccessible Superior National Forest in northeastern Minnesota, where perhaps 350 to 700 survived in the 1960s.

Soon after bounties were eliminated, wolves were protected under the federal Endangered Species Act. Numbers began to increase as wolves fed on the large number of white-tailed deer in Minnesota forests. They began to range from Superior National Forest into the western and central portions of the state. Today, about 3,000 wolves live in Minnesota.

In the photo, world-renowned wolf researcher L. David Mech tracks wolves with radio telemetry in Superior National Forest. Ever the scientist, Mech has kept an objective attitude toward the wolf, as he has argued it should be protected in parts of its range

but controlled in others. The public, he says, is rarely so dispassionate. "We humans judge these creatures by our own standards," he writes in his book *The Arctic Wolf: Living with the Pack.* "If they kill, they are bad. If they take the old, the young, the sick, and the weak, they are good. If they mate for life, that makes them better. If they kill and eat one of their own, they are ghastly."

Yesterday's photo: Minnesota Historical Society

ELY

In the 1880s, Ely sprung from the north woods as a cluster of shacks and modest commercial buildings. The town was named for—take your pick—Arthur Ely of Cleveland, a backer of the Duluth and Iron Range Railroad, or the Reverend Edmund Franklin Ely, who came to Minnesota in 1832 as a missionary to the Anishinabe. Arthur Ely seems the more likely choice, since the railroad opened in Ely in 1888, a year after the village was platted, to haul iron ore dug on the newly discovered Vermillion Range. During the next several decades, mining sustained the town. Logging was also important. Not surprisingly, given its origins, Ely had a roughneck frontier quality.

Then, with the rise in tourism in northern Minnesota in the 1920s and 1930s, Ely found itself fortuitously located as the gateway to the great network of streams and lakes in Superior National Forest that would later become the Boundary Waters Canoe Area Wilderness. Increasing numbers of tourists brushed up against the rough edges of people who had made their living in the woods and who, until then, had been left pretty much alone.

In the late 1970s, efforts to ban motorized vehicles in the Boundary Waters ignited hard feelings that persist to this day between urban visitors and conservative townsfolk. But as the iron mines close and as the timber industry becomes more strictly regulated, tourism clearly becomes ever more important to Ely's future. On summer afternoons, cars carrying canoes line Sheridan Street, and outfitters and sporting-goods shops fill with visitors making last-minute purchases before heading into the wilderness.

Yesterday's photo: Minnesota Historical Society

MINNESOTA HOCKEY

Bruce A. Noyes takes a breather from pond hockey in this 1954 photo. In Minnesota, more than in almost any other state, children spent long days on frozen ponds and local outdoor hockey rinks, banging pucks back and forth, and speeding along on ice that could be as rutted as a dirt road or as smooth as, well, ice! All they needed was a stick and skates. Even the puck was optional, sometimes replaced by any suitably sized object—even, by one account, snuff cans wrapped with tape. The games went on for hours, players coming and going depending on when meals were served and what the family had planned for the day. When finally the winter sun set and the puck could longer be seen, the game broke up with promises to return the next day.

The scene today has often shifted indoors, to regulation arenas and organized games of youth hockey, high school leagues, and, of course, university teams, including the University of Minnesota Golden Gophers, the University of Minnesota–Duluth Bulldogs, and the St. Cloud State University Huskies. On the pro scene, the Minnesota North Stars broke fans' hearts when they were sold and moved to Dallas (of all places!). But now crowds cheer-on the Minnesota Wild, whose former goalie, Dwayne Roloson, is pictured here, poised with all the armor a pro hockey player can muster.

One of the most famous Minnesota hockey players of all time was the late Herb Brooks. Born in St. Paul, he played for the United States in the Olympics and was coach to the U.S. team that pulled off the 1980 "miracle on ice" victory over the Soviet Union and then went on to win Olympic gold.

Yesterday's photo: Minnesota Historical Society

Tobie's Cafe and Bus Stop—Hinckley, Minn— A-600?

TOBIE'S

obie's Eat Shop & Bus Stop (now named Tobie's Restaurant & Bakery) capitalized on its location in Hinckley, a popular wayside town halfway between the Twin Cities and Duluth. For a long time the town was best known as the site of a disastrous forest fire in 1894 that killed more than 400 people. A café and bus stop had started on the corner Main Street and Old Highway 61 back in 1920. In 1947 (shortly before the photo was taken), "Tobie" Lackner bought the place, renamed it, and expanded it. Local residents and travelers began taking notice. The ovens of the little restaurant daily produced up to 300 dozen doughnuts, 100 dozen sweet rolls, and 60 pies.

Construction of the new Interstate 35 on the edge of town during the mid-1960s meant the restaurant would have to move to survive. In 1966, the Lackners decided to sell rather than relocate. John Schrade bought the restaurant and moved it nearer the freeway. Despite subsequent changes in ownership, the restaurant has continued to thrive. It still is known best for its caramel rolls and it still bills itself as "Minnesota's Famous Halfway Stop."

Yesterday's photo: Minnesota Historical Society

"Look! What a Peach I Landed — and How!"

Great Sport fishing here.

Copyright 1910 by Hanson Post Card Co.

Here's just a sample. The rest were so heavy that I had to leave 'em behind.

WHATTAMAN!

GREETINGS FROM ELY, MINN.

THE KIND WE CATCH.   PEQUOT, MINN.,

GREETINGS FROM ROSEAU, MINN.

The Fish Here are a little Hard to Land

FISHING

The Land of 10,000 Lakes actually claims 11,842 lakes that are 10 acres or larger, and several thousand miles of rivers and streams. So you'd expect that fishing and tall tales about fishing would have been popular ever since Anishinabe gathered around a fire at the end of a day. The angler's art of stretching the truth found an outlet in the photo postcards of the early and mid-1900s, which were sold in bait shops, hotels, restaurants, gift shops, and other tourist hangouts all over the state.

In some ways, fishing really was better in the good old days. In 1911, Minnesota began to sell fishing licenses to nonresidents for $1.00. Resident fishing licenses first went on sale in 1927. The number sold has increased every year, on average, despite a depression and two world wars. After World War II, the boom in leisure time, travel, and highway construction caused fishing to boom. Today, Minnesota has about 3.5 anglers for every one angler back in the 1920s. More than 2.3 million anglers (that includes licensed anglers and children who are not required to buy licenses) fish in Minnesota each year. With more crowds and more fishing pressure, some fish—trophy northern pike, for example—are much rarer than they used to be.

On the other hand, more people are practicing catch and release. Fisheries management has advanced. Some waters, such as the trout streams of the southeast, have improved with better conservation practices. So for some kinds of fishing, for some species, these days *are* the good old days.

Minnesota currently ranks first in the nation for sales of fishing licenses per capita. Anglers, including those who fish from a modern fishing boat on Lake Vermilion, a canoe in the Boundary Waters Canoe Area, or a dock on the edge of a metropolitan lake, catch mostly sunfish, followed by walleye (the state fish), and northern pike.

Yesterday's photos: Voyageur Press archives

ALL-WEATHER ANGLERS

Two proud anglers congratulate each other on their catch of smallmouth bass and walleyes (or possibly saugers), photographed in 1913 before a studio's pastoral backdrop. To the outdoorsman, whether he lived on a farm in central Minnesota or traveled here from the eastern United States, Minnesota meant good fishing. Most folks have taken that to mean relaxing with a bobber and long pole on a sunny summer day. But from the beginning, die-hard anglers have pursued their sport year-round. It's hard to argue with the result of early ice-fishermen, but over the years, tactics and gear have become more sophisticated. Now it's possible to go fishing on frozen Lake Harriet in Minneapolis while keeping up with your work on a laptop. With better transportation (such as snowmobiles), better clothing, and better equipment (such as power ice augers), ice fishing has become ever more popular. At the annual Brainerd Jaycees Ice-Fishing Extravaganza, 13,000 anglers spread out on the ice of Gull Lake to pursue prizes of trucks, snowmobiles, and cash for catching the largest fish.

Yesterday's photos: Minnesota Historical Society; Voyageur Press archives

GREAT NORTHERN PIKE
A FEW 10 TO 20 POUNDERS FROM PEQUOT, MINN.

MINNEAPOLIS MILL DISTRICT

Minneapolis grew along the sprawling Mississippi River waterfront. In fact, without St. Anthony Falls, the city would have had no reason to exist. Soldiers from Fort Snelling built a sawmill on the west bank of the falls in 1821, and the first flour mill was built nearby two years later. Soon sawmills and flour mills grew along both sides of the river. The river's east bank (actually the northeast bank) became known as St. Anthony, while the other bank grew to be known as Minneapolis. The competing settlements were brought together as "Minneapolis" in 1872.

The natural waterfall of St. Anthony was unstable. Water tumbling over the hard limestone caprock eroded the soft layer of sandstone underneath. Periodically, the limestone layer would break and collapse. Attempts to excavate channels through the rock to draw off additional water contributed to the instability. In 1869, much of the falls collapsed, destroying many mills in the process.

The following decade might be known as the age of disaster. In addition to the collapse of the falls, fire destroyed the east side of the dam and east bank sawmills. The financial panic of 1873 injured all businesses. An explosion and fire in 1878 destroyed much of the west bank milling district. Nonetheless, flour-milling recovered and prospered. For a half century, Minneapolis was known as the Flour Milling Capital of the World. The Washburn A Mill was one of the most advanced mills in existence, grinding in a single day enough Gold Medal Flour for 12 million bread loaves.

Other major industries were barrel-making and the manufacture of prosthetics (to replace limbs lost in mill accidents).

After World War I, the milling industry in Minneapolis declined. As the industry moved out of Minneapolis, the old mills fell into disuse. The Washburn A Mill closed in 1965 and was nearly destroyed by fire in 1991.

Today, the Minnesota Historical Society's Mill City Museum, built inside the remains of the Washburn A Mill, tells the story of Minneapolis's milling industry. And the riverfront along the concrete-reinforced falls has been renovated with restaurants, stores, parks, and trails.

Yesterday's photos: Library of Congress; Voyageur Press archives

M-92—Streamliner Crossing Mississippi River over Stone Arch Bridge, Minneapolis, Minn.

STONE ARCH BRIDGE

At the height of the milling industry in Minneapolis, up to eighty trains a day crossed the graceful Stone Arch Bridge, bringing grain to mills and leaving with flour and other manufactured goods. Built in 1882–1883, the bridge consists of twenty-three arches forming a graceful curve 2,100 feet long a few hundred yards below St. Anthony Falls. The bridge not only carried the vital cargo of Minneapolis; it also stood as a monument to its builder, railroad magnate James J. Hill. It is constructed of locally quarried Platteville limestone, St. Cloud granite, and limestone from Stone City, Iowa. Hill, ever the perfectionist, was said to have been angry over the quality of stone he could obtain for his bridge. And so he bought a quarry to be able to directly supervise the mining.

When locks were built around St. Anthony Falls in the early 1960s, two bridge arches and one pier near the lock channel were replaced with a steel truss. The bridge continued to carry trains until 1965.

In 1975, the bridge was designated a National Historic Civil Engineering Landmark. Twenty years later, after extensive refurbishing, the bridge was opened to pedestrians, skaters, bikers, and trolleys—a monument to the future of a livable city. Today the bridge offers a striking view of town, including the ruins of several old mills, reminders of the industry that built Minneapolis.

Yesterday's photos: Voyageur Press archives

Great Northern Viaduct, Flour Milling District and
St. Anthony Falls, Minneapolis.

MINNEAPOLIS SKYLINE

The cluster of buildings identified as "A Bunch of Sky Scrapers" in this 1910 postcard would hardly warrant the name even a few years later. The spire on the right belonged to the Minneapolis City Hall, 341 feet tall when completed in 1906. It reigned as the tallest building in the city until 1929, when the Foshay Tower was completed. The city hall's terra-cotta roof was replaced by a copper roof in the 1950s. The building was added to the National Register of Historic Places in 1974.

Today, though it has been overshadowed by much taller buildings, the Richardsonian Romanesque city hall (far right) continues to stand out in the downtown landscape. The Minneapolis skyline is beautiful and buoyant, outclassing any other in the state, including the stodgy and undistinguished silhouette of St. Paul. Prominent buildings, from the left in the photo, include the Foshay Tower, the IDS Center, Wells Fargo Center, 225 South Sixth, and, in the foreground, the Hubert H. Humphrey Metrodome.

As the metropolitan area has grown upward, it has also grown outward. Though the population of Minneapolis (382,618 in 2000) has, in general, slowly declined, the population of the Twin Cities metro area has nearly doubled in the last four decades and now totals about 3 million.

Yesterday's photo: Voyageur Press archives

FOSHAY TOWER

"TALLEST BUILDING IN THE NORTHWEST"
32 STORIES   447 FEET 3 INCHES

HI! FOLKS! WE'RE IN
MINNEAPOLIS,
MINNESOTA

I CAN SEE OUR HOME TOWN FROM HERE!

FOSHAY TOWER

On 6 August 1928, the outlines of the nascent Foshay Tower were taking shape. Until this time, the Minneapolis skyline consisted almost wholly of squat, square buildings. The only office that could justify the term *skyscraper* was the 341-foot City Hall, visible in the far right of the photo.

But the Foshay was much grander than city hall, and became the pride of the city skyline for decades. When it was finished in 1929, it measured 448 feet tall, with thirty-two floors, the first skyscraper west of the Mississippi. It's builder, newly minted millionaire Wilbur Foshay, had been inspired by the Washington Monument as a child, and vowed that if he ever became rich enough, he would build an office that would resemble it.

And so he did. The headquarters of his new public utility measured 81-by-87 feet at the bottom and tapered to 59-by-65 feet near the top. It had a two-story base on three sides, clad in Indiana limestone. The Foshay Tower remains the most prominent obelisk-shaped skyscraper in existence.

The tower was dedicated in a ceremony spanning 30 August to 1 September 1929. Foshay commissioned John Philip Sousa to write a march for the tower's opening. Sousa renamed a previously written march, which was then performed at eight concerts in the city. Within two months, however, the stock market crashed. Foshay's public utility went into receivership and his $20,000 check to Sousa bounced. Sousa withheld use of his commissioned march until a group of city residents raised donations to pay his commission.

Foshay's tower was controversial. Not only did it rise above everything else in the city, it was constructed with all-union labor at a time of labor unrest and repression. Nonetheless, for decades the building—with FOSHAY spelled out in 10-foot-high letters lit by 976 60-watt bulbs—defined the Minneapolis skyline. It remained the city's tallest building until the construction of the IDS Tower in 1973, and it was added to the National Register of Historic Places in 1977.

And Foshay himself? He was tried for mail and securities fraud, convicted in 1932, and sentenced to Leavenworth Penitentiary. He served three years before President Franklin Roosevelt commuted his sentence. Foshay died in a Minneapolis nursing home in 1957.

Yesterday's photos: Minnesota Historical Society; Voyageur Press archives

M-64 SKYLINE, MINNEAPOLIS, MINN.

CITY OF LAKES AND PARKS   SA-H1892

HENNEPIN AVENUE

In this photo at left, traffic plows through slush on Hennepin Avenue between Sixth and Seventh streets in February 1953. Hennepin Avenue, named for the Belgian priest who laid eyes on St. Anthony Falls in 1679, slices through the city from north to south, joining the old St. Anthony milling district on the northeast side of the Mississippi, and then running past Loring Park and the Walker Art Center to Uptown and south Minneapolis. Through downtown, it has always been known as the city's entertainment street—though the type of entertainment found there has changed with the economy and the city's fortunes. At the time of this photo, respectable theaters and bars have given way to porn shops and strip clubs.

The Gopher Theatre is no more. It opened in 1911 as the Grand, a vaudeville house. Remodeled in the 1930s as the Gopher, it lasted into the 1970s, when it began to show porn. It closed in 1979 and was subsequently torn down.

Most of the businesses around the Gopher in 1953 have since gone under, but not Shinder's, a major presence on the avenue since 1916, when Shinder brothers Al and Harry bought a newsstand on the avenue. Younger brothers Hy, Daniel, and Bill soon joined them. They prospered through the vaudeville era, the Depression, and World War II, selling newspapers to gangsters, cops, politicians, theater stars, and union officials. Several times a day, the Shinders would pick up the latest newspaper editions at the post office or train station. During the war, they were selling up to 3,000 newspapers and 900 magazines daily, twenty-four hours a day. Over the years, they have continued to become ever more eclectic, selling everything from comics to porn to classics.

Hennepin was in a period of decline when the city decided to renovate so-called Block E on the west side of the avenue. The redeveloped block has restaurants, retail, theaters, and other entertainment. Shinder's is now located one block south of its original location.

Yesterday's photo: Minnesota Historical Society

NICOLLET AVENUE

Long before Mary Tyler Moore was born, and certainly well before she famously flung her hat in the air while strolling the Nicollet Mall near Seventh Street, Nicollet Avenue became the primary shopping street in Minneapolis with the opening of such stores as Powers (1881), Donaldson's (1884), Young Quinlan (1894), and Dayton's (1902). Retail, and Nicollet Avenue itself, remained vital into the mid-century. Then, in an effort to reinvigorate the downtown shopping district as shoppers turned toward the suburbs, the avenue was converted to Nicollet Mall, a mile-long walkway curving through downtown. Lined by sidewalks, fountains, sculptures, and trees, it is closed to automobiles (but do watch out for buses). Strolling down the mall in summer or winter, you're never far from the city's 5-mile-long system of heated and elevated skyways. Among the attractions on the mall today are upscale stores, shops, and restaurants. A farmers' market sells produce in summer. The city's popular Holidazzle parade proceeds along the mall in winter. And

at Seventh Avenue is a bronze statue of Mary Tyler Moore, tossing her hat aloft.

Yesterday's photos: Voyageur Press archives

Nicollet Avenue from Ninth Street, Minneapolis, Minn.

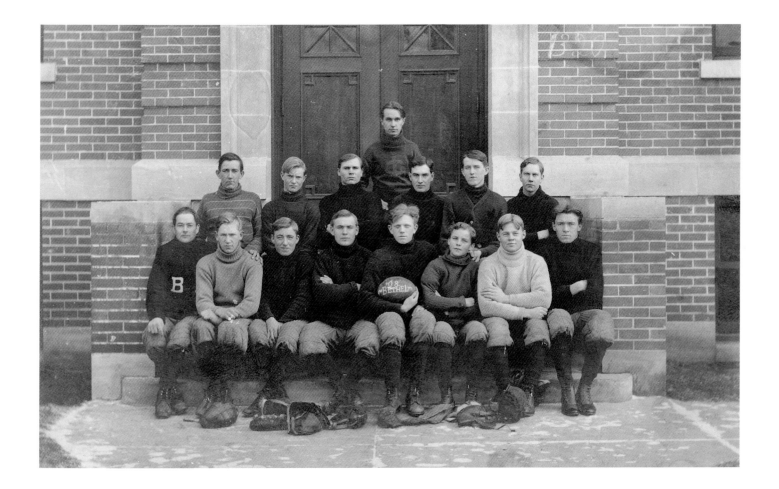

MINNESOTA FOOTBALL

Perhaps when the 1908 Bethel collegiate team posed for this photograph, the Twin Cities were already becoming a "football town." In 1882, the University of Minnesota, in its first game, beat Hamline 4–0. A couple of years later, two Minnesota rugby players combined a Dakota battle cry with a shortening of the university's name for the collegiate yell *Sky-U-Mah*.

Certainly football fervor was growing in 1924, when Memorial Stadium opened its archways to fans of University of Minnesota football. And it must have been at fever pitch during the years 1934–1941, when Bernie Bierman coached the Minnesota Golden Gophers to five national championships, and in 1962 when All-American Sandy Stephens led the Golden Gophers to their only Rose Bowl victory.

The Gophers still draw a crowd, but these days Minnesotans are *pro* football fans, rising and falling on the fortunes of the Minnesota Vikings. The Vikings played their first game in 1961 at old Metropolitan Stadium in Bloomington. Coach Norm Van Brocklin and rookie quarterback Fran Tarkenton led the Vikes to a 37–13 win over the Chicago Bears. Since then, the Vikings made runs at Super Bowl championships in 1969, 1973, 1974, and 1976, but lost each time under legendary coach Bud Grant. Fans bide their time for another appearance, cheered on by mascot "Ragnar" the Viking, otherwise known as Joseph Juranitch.

Yesterday's photo: Voyageur Press archives

DOWNTOWN EATERIES

Through World War II, the Casablanca Café and Bar, 408 Hennepin, drew crowds with lunch specials during the day and jazz bands in the evening. By accounts, it was a popular spot with servicemen and other hard-drinking folks leaving piles of cigarettes at the bar rail. Noisy groups of men and women jammed together at small round tables to listen to music. On 21 July 1944, during a time of radical politics among unions (and just ten years after the deadly Minneapolis truckers' strike), an organizer for General Drivers and Helpers Union 544 was shot and killed after a violent fight in the Casablanca at 2:30 A.M. In the years since, both crime and the Casablanca itself have faded into the mists.

Other storefront eateries from that era have persevered. Murray's, established on Sixth Street in 1946, became known as the "Home of the Silver Butter Knife Steak." A third-generation of the Murray family still runs the downtown landmark.

Yesterday's photos: Minnesota Historical Society; Voyageur Press archives

MINNEAPOLIS–ST. PAUL AIRPORT

In 1949, the Twin Cities airport had just added international flights and so took the name Minneapolis-St. Paul International Airport (MSP). The facility sat on the site of the old Snelling Speedway, overlooking the Minnesota River. The racetrack had long gone out of business but had been purchased in 1914 by the Minneapolis Aero Club.

The first hangar was built of wood in 1920, the same year the first runway was constructed. In 1923, the airport was named Wold-Chamberlain Field to honor Ernest Wold and Cyrus Chamberlain, local pilots killed in combat in World War I. In 1926, Northwest Airways won the government's airmail contract and purchased the sole hangar. The airline consisted of two rented open-cockpit biplanes that carried mail between the Twin Cities and Chicago. In 1927, Northwest served 106 passengers—one-fourth the capacity of a Boeing 747.

The new Lindbergh Terminal, named for the Minnesotan who became the first person to fly solo across the Atlantic, was opened in 1962. Within five years, it served more than 4.1 million passengers a year. Passenger use continued to exceed expectations; to keep up, the Humphrey Terminal was added and nearly all other airport facilities were expanded.

In 2004, Minneapolis–St. Paul International Airport accommodated more than 36 million passengers and more than a half-million takeoffs and landings—ranking MSP ninth for passenger use among North American airports.

Northwest Airlines has long been known for service to East Asia. In 1947, flights hopped from the Twin Cities to Edmonton in Canada; to Anchorage and Shemya in Alaska; and then farther east to such cities as Tokyo, Seoul, Shanghai, and Manila. In 1970, Northwest began flying Boeing 747s to Asia, as it continues to do today.

Yesterday's photo: Voyageur Press archives

CITY RAILS

In the 1920s, a conductor collected fares on a Twin Cities streetcar top left.

Street railways began operating in St. Paul in 1872, and in Minneapolis in 1875. At first the cars were drawn by horses, then they were powered by steam, and finally by electricity. In 1892, the street railways in both cities were unified into the Twin City Rapid Transit Co., renowned as one of the most efficient metropolitan transit systems in the country.

Streetcar service peaked about 1920, providing 220 million rides a year—about four times the volume of today's metro transit system. Even then, however, bus systems were competing with streetcars along many of the same routes. The replacement of streetcars with buses began in the late 1930s.

In the photo, a streetcar squeezes through Fourth Street East and Robert Street in St. Paul, on 11 May 1950. By this time, streetcars were clearly on their way out. Buses provided more flexible routing, and the rising use of autos cut into the overall demand for public transit. Buses replaced the last Twin Cities streetcars in 1954. The following spring, St. Paul tore up the tracks at Fourth Street and Wabasha Avenue.

Apparently urban rail is an idea that has come and gone—and come back again. In June 2004, light rail began service along the Hiawatha Line between downtown Minneapolis and Fort Snelling, and soon after, to Minneapolis–St. Paul International Airport and the Mall of America. By 2005, the line carried more than 19,000 passengers on a typical weekday. Both Minneapolis and St. Paul have considered reviving streetcar lines along city streets.

Yesterday's photos: Minnesota Historical Society

STREETS AND SKYWAYS

As Minneapolis and St. Paul grew, their bustling streets filled with people and vehicles. In winter, icy blasts and snow made travel difficult for pedestrians and vehicles. (In the early days, people resorted to horse-drawn sleighs on downtown streets.) It took a few years to find a solution to winter transportation woes, but in 1962, Minneapolis unveiled its first skyway, an enclosed walkway a full story above street level.

Businessman Leslie Park is credited with inventing the skyway system. Since the early 1950s, he had been trying to sell the idea to the downtown community. Park finally made an impression on the City Planning Department, which commissioned Park to develop a plan for the system. The first skyway linked the Northstar Center to what is now the Wells Fargo Center. The skyway was an immediate tourist attraction, and second-floor real estate increased in value. St. Paul followed suit in 1967, with a skyway linking the Federal Courts Building to the Pioneer Press Building.

Both cities continue to build skyways. In Minneapolis, the walkways are designed, owned, and paid for by building owners. The structures have shown more design innovation than in St. Paul, where the skyways are publicly owned and standardized. Either way, each city now has about 5 miles of skyways connecting downtown buildings, so that pedestrians can navigate the loop without having to brave snow or winter winds.

Yesterday's photos: Voyageur Press archives

MINNESOTA BASEBALL

In this photo at left taken in 1935, one of the years the minor-league Minneapolis Millers won a championship, an outfielder for the Millers leaps for the camera, as if to make a catch.

Minnesota's baseball goes back to the mid-1800s, when amateur teams were organized in cities throughout the state. In 1884, the professional Northwestern League came to Minnesota, with teams in Minneapolis, St. Paul, Stillwater, and Winona. But this was a time of flux in baseball, as teams and leagues went out of business and new teams formed only briefly.

In 1902, the Minneapolis Millers and St. Paul Saints found some stability in the new minor-league American Association. The two teams played in the league for fifty-nine seasons—the Millers at Nicollet Park and the Saints in Lexington Park (and later, Midway). During that time, the Saints fielded several future

Hall of Famers, including Lefty Gomez, Duke Snider, and Roy Campanella. The Millers were even more blessed with talent, with Ted Williams, Willie Mays, and Carl Yastrzemski.

Other pro and semi-pro teams played in Minnesota as well. The Minneapolis Millerettes of the All-American Girls Professional Baseball League played their only season in Minnesota in 1945. Two all-black teams to play were the St. Paul Gophers and the Minneapolis Keystones.

The days of the Millers and Saints ended after the 1960 season, when Calvin Griffith announced he would move his Washington Senators to Minnesota. Starting in 1961, Minnesota had a major-league team.

With the likes of Harmon Killebrew, Bob Allison, and Jim Kaat, the new Minnesota Twins quickly found success. By 1965, they had won the American League pennant and had lost to the

Los Angeles Dodgers in a series of seven World Series games.

The Twins went indoors with the opening of the Hubert H. Humphrey Metrodome in 1982. In 1987, the Twins beat the St. Louis Cardinals to win the World Series. They won the series again in 1991—beating the Atlanta Braves with an extra-innings homerun by Kirby Puckett to win game six, and heroic pitching by Jack Morris to win game seven.

Despite the success of the Twins, minor league made a resurgence. In 1993, a new St. Paul Saints team began playing in the open air of Midway Stadium. Ila Borders (photo above), the first woman to play in a men's professional league, played for both the Saints and the Duluth minor-league team, the Duluth Dukes.

Yesterday's photos: Minnesota Historical Society; Voyageur Press archives

EDINA

In 1939, cars and street cars vied for space on 50th Street and France Avenue, the developing commercial district of Edina. Bordering the southwest corner of Minneapolis, the community withdrew from Richfield Township in a dispute over highways and taxes. Edina was incorporated in 1888 and named by its Scotch-Irish residents after one of two grist mills in the community, the Edina Mills, which, in turn, had been named after the city of Edinburgh, Scotland.

Over the years, Edina has grown into a prosperous community known primarily for its wealth, expensive homes, and country clubs. The corner of 50th and France has become a classic urban shopping neighborhood, with theaters, restaurants, and tony shops. Yet the classic urbanism of this little enclave is the antithesis of the area that truly distinguishes Edina historically and architecturally: Southdale. Located a mile south on France Avenue, Southdale was the first entirely enclosed shopping center in the United States. Conceived by the Dayton family, owners of the area's most prestigious department store, Southdale opened October 7, 1956. Twin Cities residents had their pick of seventy stores on two levels surrounding a central court. Once inside, patrons could shop all day without exposure to winter winds. As a press release announcing the opening said, "No matter what the weatherman says, it's always spring at Southdale." And parking was free. When it came time to find their cars, shoppers could follow the animal signs—"Now, was I parked in the giraffe lot, the elephant lot, or the kangaroo lot?"

Yesterday's photo: Minneapolis Public Library

GAS STATIONS

Since George Hartzell pumped gas at this Edina location in the 1920s top left, service stations have changed almost as much as the vehicles they serve. In 1956, "full service" at this Phillips 66 at bottom left, an undisclosed location apparently meant two attendants per car, wiping windshields and checking tires.

As the pumps, buildings, and lots have grown fancier, convenience stores have replaced service stations. Rarely do attendants meet you at the pump. Imagine the owner of a Model T pulling up to Bobby and Steve's Auto World Gas Station in downtown Minneapolis. Gas, auto repair, twenty-four-hour towing, a "touch-free" tunnel car wash, and an all-hours convenience store, with Dunn Bros. coffee!

But where's the guy to check the oil?

Yesterday's photos: Minneapolis Public Library; Minnesota Historical Society

CINEMAS

In fall 1929, the Nokomis theater, at 3749 Chicago Avenue South in Minneapolis, announced the coming of its first "talkie," the baseball comedy *Fast Company*. The theater was then showing *The Flying Marine*, which closed out an era of silent films.

The years have not been kind to many small neighborhood and downtown theaters. The Nokomis, for example, closed; in 1987, it was converted to an auto-body-repair shop (the stage area is now a paint booth). Other neighborhood movie houses have similar stories, including the Boulevard, Camden, Minnesota, and Metropolitan, Palace, Nile theaters in Minneapolis, and the Paramount and Princess theaters in St. Paul. All were closed and gutted or demolished.

The Time is a case in point. The small 250-seat art-deco house opened at 729 Hennepin Avenue in downtown Minneapolis as a first-run theater. By the time of the photograph, taken in 1938, the Time was showing second-run films, such as Alfred Lunt and Lynn Fontanne in *The Guardsman*. Soon after, the Time became

the Esquire and began showing adult films. It ran afoul of police with the Sally Rand flick *Nude Ranch* (authorities insisted the marquee be changed to "Dude Ranch"). During the 1940s, the Esquire became the Newsreel and began showing wartime newsreels; it later became the Pix, was closed in 1952, and was ultimately converted to retail space.

Perhaps because the auto has allowed us to wander farther afield for shopping and entertainment, movie theaters have since spread out and become larger, with multiple screens. The epitome of the trend, at least for the moment, is the Lakeville 18 Theatre. Nonetheless, some downtown and neighborhood movie houses have survived as theaters of one kind or another. The Mann Grandview in St. Paul shows first-run films. The Avalon on East Lake Street houses Heart of the Beast puppet theater. In Columbia Heights, the Heights has been fully restored to its Roaring Twenties glory. The Fitzgerald Theater, built in 1910 as the Sam S. Shubert, is home to the *Prairie Home Companion* radio show and is the oldest surviving theater space in downtown St. Paul.

Yesterday's photos: Minnesota Historical Society

GROCERY STORES

ost of the clerks in the top left photo don't quite manage a smile as they pose in an unnamed St. Paul grocery story in 1900. The number of personnel suggests a wealth of personal service, even though the stock, albeit with plenty of locally grown vegetables and freshly baked goods, might be a bit limited by present standards.

In 1956, a young clerk shows off a bag of Red River spuds at a Red Owl store at an undisclosed location. Over the years, the local grocery industry has undergone various dislocations. Of the familiar names of yesteryear—Applebaums, National Tea, Piggly Wiggly, Red Owl, Super Valu, and a host of independently owned stores—some have survived, some have vanished, some have morphed into something new.

For the most part, grocery stores have consolidated and grown larger, like most everything else in retail. At the same time, foodstuffs are transported ever greater distances, are packaged in new ways, and are more varied than ever before. A Byerly's in St. Louis Park offers an example of a modern, high-end grocery store, emphasizing service and pleasant surroundings.

But a few stores hark back to grocers of yesteryear—or they never changed in the first place. The Bay Store on Lake of the Woods, near the Canadian border, has been serving its faithful customers for decades, in the fashion of the old-time general store.

Yesterday's photos: Minnesota Historical Society

GENERAL STORES AND THE MALL OF AMERICA

Atwater's main drag in 1890 reflects the retail sensibilities of the day—independent specialty stores arrayed along a boardwalk and a muddy street. The general store of the time attempted to provide one-stop shopping. And the big-city department stores, such as Powers, Donaldson's, and Dayton's in Minneapolis, made a serious attempt to offer everything the shopper might need or want. With the debut of the shopping mall, retailers created a space that reflected the varied main street of old, with lines of specialty shops—but they put them all together under one roof. Southdale in Edina, the nation's first enclosed mall, started the trend in 1956. Others soon followed: Brookdale, Rosedale, Ridgedale, and others. The ultimate expression of the mall, at least in Minnesota, has been the Mall of America.

Since it opened in 1992, the Mall of America has become a favorite with local shoppers and a draw to out-of-staters, attracting 40 million visitors annually. Its 4.2 million square feet include a 7-acre indoor theme park with more than thirty rides and attractions and nine places to eat; department stores, including Nordstrom, Macy's, Bloomingdale's, and Sears; more than 400 specialty stores; and bars, restaurants, and nightclubs. Underwater Adventures is an inside-out mega aquarium, in which visitors walk down a 300-foot-long tunnel surrounded by more than a million gallons of water harboring 4,500 sea creatures, including colorful reef fish and menacing sharks.

Yesterday's photo: Minnesota Historical Society

ONE OF THE FIVE BETTY CROCKER KITCHENS
AT GENERAL MILLS, MINNEAPOLIS, MINN.

MINNESOTA WOMEN

A postcard from the early 1900s portrays the "Minnesota Belle," bottom left, the feminine ideal in upper Midwest wheat country, complete with a cozy farmhouse and the state seal (of a farmer watching an Indian on horseback vanish into the sunset).

Perhaps the most famous fictional feminine role model from Minnesota is Betty Crocker. Betty was created by flour giant Washburn Crosby Co. of Minneapolis (later to become General Mills) to give a more personal touch to the company's many responses to baking question. Betty's hair and clothes have changed to reflect the current style. And her face has morphed to better represent the company's customers. From the time of her first portrait in 1936 to her most recent update sixty years later, Betty has evolved from a rather tight-lipped Anglo with gray curls, to a younger, darker, and more cheerful spokeswoman.

Today, we imagine woman to be more athletic and adventurous than they once were. Minnesota explorer Ann Bancroft trains near Scandia for crossing the Antarctic on skis. Bancroft has made history with expeditions to both poles. Yet there's room for traditional roles: Former Miss Minnesota USA Melissa Hall, now a fitness model, appears at a St. Paul Saints baseball game with team mascot Hamlet the pig.

Despite Minnesota's reputation for liberal politics, the state has never elected a woman as governor or as U.S. senator. In fact, it has elected only two to the U.S. House of Representatives: Coya Knutson in 1954 and Betty McCollum in 2000.

Yesterday's photos: Voyageur Press archives

MINNEHAHA FALLS

A man paused in his walk across the footbridge below Minnehaha Falls in Minneapolis in about 1900. A postcard from the same era shows the falls frozen in winter. The perspective is the familiar overlook in Minnehaha Park, one of the city's oldest and most popular parks, which attracts over a million visitors a year. The falls, measuring about 53 feet high, are one of the city's signature landmarks.

The falls formed in the last several thousand years as St. Anthony Falls on the Mississippi, once much farther downstream than it is today, eroded the underlying sandstone bedrock and retreated upstream step-by-step, leaving behind a deeply eroded gorge that Minnehaha Creek simply plunged into, forming the waterfall.

The falls was dubbed Brown's Falls after army officer Jacob Brown. The Dakota called it simply *haha*, a waterfall, as they did other waterfalls. Missionary Samuel W. Pond Jr. noted that European settlers apparently joined the Dakota words *minne* (water) and *haha* (falls). "The Indians never knew it by the latter name," Pond reported. The name and the site achieved widespread recognition from Longfellow's 1855 poem "The Song of Hiawatha."

The area was once a busy train stop. In 1889, the state loaned the city of Minneapolis $100,000 to purchase the park from its

Minneapolis, Minn., Minnehaha Falls.

private owners. The park, of course, was given the poetic name of its beautiful waterfall—a memento, in a way, of the land's original settlers.

Yesterday's photos: Voyageur Press archives

Photograph © Wayne Kryduba

About the Authors

Educated in fine art photography, Layne Kennedy's editorial images blend art and information. His images have been published worldwide on subjects as varied as wolves in Minnesota to pink dolphins in the Amazon River. His feature work appears regularly in *Smithsonian, Life, Audubon, Sports Illustrated, Nature Conservancy, Newsweek, National Geographic Traveler, National Geographic Adventure, Outside,* and other magazines. He has photographed books for the National Geographic Society and Voyageur Press. He lives in Minneapolis with his wife and three children.

Despite his best intentions to do otherwise, Greg Breining has lived in Minnesota his entire life. He has written several books about the state and region. His articles and essays have appeared in *Sports Illustrated, National Geographic Adventure, Audubon, Wildlife Conservation, Minnesota Conservation Volunteer,* and other magazines. He lives in St. Paul with his wife, Susan Binkley.

We Caught A Few Small Ones Today

Just as big fish in the se
were caught? Well, I'm
om now.
GREETINGS FROM GLENWO

M-81—Wold-Chamberlain Field, St. Paul-Minneapolis, Minn.

Main Driveway inside of W
Minnesota State Prison, Stillwat

Silver Creek Cliff and Lake Shore Drive

Lake Superior 383 mi. long, 160 wide
1200 ft deep, tide 3"

M-52 NEW POST OFFICE.